PRAISE FOR PERSONALIZATION A

CW00746863

'It's unusual to land a job that was designed for you, but it's possible to tailor a job into one that suits you. Job crafting is a skill that every employee needs and every manager should value, and this is the first book to bring the research and practice together in an engaging and accessible way for HR professionals.'
Adam Grant, *New York Times* bestselling author of *Originals* and *Give and Take*, and host of the chart-topping TED podcast *WorkLife*

'*Personalization at Work* through job crafting is a unique and innovative book. For too long we have heard HR professionals say "our most valuable resource is our human resource", something that should translate into helping employees personalize their work to enable them to get a good balance in their lives – but hasn't in the past. This is a must-read for those concerned about enabling their people to thrive.'
Professor Sir Cary Cooper, Alliance Manchester Business School, University of Manchester

'The world of work is in a more dissatisfied place than in any previous generation. Job crafting represents a massive opportunity for all of us to achieve a personalization revolution in our work. Finally this could be the way to make our jobs more rewarding and joyful than ever before.'
Bruce Daisley, author of *The Joy of Work*, and former VP – Europe, Twitter

'*Personalization at Work* is a valuable asset to human resource managers, workplace leaders, organizational scholars and, most importantly, anyone who wants to have a thriving career. Rob Baker provides us with a compelling reason to personalize our work and helps us to more clearly understand the factors that prevent us from doing so.

The chapters on job crafting offer practical ideas for how workplaces can organize jobs to provide choice, opportunity and energy. Given the amount of time people spend at work, Baker's invitation to craft jobs in ways that foster thriving is powerful. His book will herald a new way to work and it can't come soon enough. This is a must-read!'
Professor Lea Waters, Organizational Psychologist, positive psychology expert, and author of *The Strength Switch*

'Rob Baker has written an important, progressive and practical book. I recommend it to anyone aspiring to a working life that is both more productive and more fulfilling.'
Matthew Taylor, Chief Executive, RSA

'Job crafting is a validated process for enhancing the meaningfulness of work, and evidence is strong that performance increases markedly when job crafting is implemented. Rob Baker has written the best book yet on what job crafting entails, how to implement it, and what results can be expected. This is a must-read for anyone interested in helping employees and organizations flourish.'
Kim Cameron, William Russell Professor of Management and Organizations, Ross School of Business

'This is an important and fascinating account of a key issue in contemporary workplaces – how to customize our jobs so that they meet our changing needs. Drawing on dated principles of scientific management, many jobs are inflexible and adopt a one-size-fits-all approach. Baker presents a compelling argument as to why this is no longer fit for purpose and takes us through how to explore, experiment with, encourage and embed job crafting in ways that meet individual and organizational needs. Resulting in improved engagement, wellbeing and performance, job crafting is widely relevant and explored in depth in this book.'
Carol Atkinson, Professor of HRM, Centre for Decent Work and Productivity, Manchester Metropolitan University Business School

'This book makes a compelling case for the need to personalize HR and management practices to enhance employee wellbeing and performance. It is a much needed antidote to the naive assumption that universal solutions can be found in the world of work or beyond. People are unique, so it's our task to find the right unique approach for dealing with them and unlocking their potential.'
Tomas Chamorro-Premuzic, Professor of Business Psychology, UCL and Columbia and Chief Talent Scientist, manpowergroup

'For many of us work has become more than just a way to earn a living. Rob Baker has created a handbook for those yearning for more meaning and purpose at work.

Our work has never defined us more than it does today and the future of work has never been more uncertain. Rather than striving to work for the best companies, maybe it's time we strived to be the best employees. This book will help you do just that. Job and skills crafting is part of our future that many of us have yet to concentrate on.

Personalization at Work challenges the old way we think about work and teaches us to build better careers for us and our teams. A must-read for the future of work and what it means to us.'
Gethin Nadin, Director of Wellbeing, Benefex, and author of *A World of Good: Lessons from around the world in improving the employee experience*

'Rob Baker has put forth something that all organizations have been longing for – a way to stay relevant, viable and attractive to both employees and the marketplace. I agree with him that job crafting and personalization are needed in today's workplace and the workplace of the future. I will be using the concepts from this book as an essential part of my HR/business library.'
Steve Browne, SHRM-SCP, VP of Human Resources, LaRosa's, Inc, and author of *HR on Purpose*

'Rob Baker has given me, and the profession I've come to love working in (HR), a huge step into the true future of work. Not the hype we get presented with via media sound bites, but in the personalization of work and the need to bring job crafting into people's working lives.

Job and role design have been mechanized, work-by-numbers approaches, way past their sell-by date, but no one has conceived the next stage in designing roles until now. Whilst I'm a huge believer in self-managed enterprises, Rob Baker gives us an alternative: self-designed jobs. This really IS the future of work – people designing in harmony with HR professionals to build roles that play to their strengths, stretch them to learn and deliver value to the organizations they work with.

It's not that the future of work is human – it already is that. The future of work is personalization.'
Perry Timms, Founder and Chief Energy Officer, People and Transformational HR Ltd, and author of *Transformational HR*

'In *Personalization at Work*, Rob Baker has created a handbook for success and wellbeing in the modern workplace. The message is clear: the future of work is personal. This is THE definitive guide to job crafting and the many benefits it can bring to you and your business.'
Mark Gilroy, Managing Director, TMS Development International Ltd

'*Personalization at Work* is compelling, informative and thought provoking. It is very timely as the next generation of employees are more demanding of meaning and purpose and job crafting is a key part of the solution to providing a more rewarding experience for all of us. Many of us will be working later in life than our predecessors so this book is a must-read to ensure we do that in as enjoyable and productive a way as possible. As a concept it is a win-win all round.'
Roisin Currie, People and Retail Director, Greggs plc

'So much has been attempted by organizations to instil a sense of purpose in the working lives of employees at a macro level. Have we been missing a trick all along? Supported by some eye-opening insights, *Personalization at Work* provides a practical guide to how organizations can help individuals find greater purpose in their work at a personalized level, through job crafting. Surely a worthwhile pursuit for any organization that truly values its people.'
John Ryder, Founder and CEO, Hive.HR

Personalization at Work

*How HR can use job crafting to drive
performance, engagement and wellbeing*

Rob Baker

KoganPage

Publisher's note

Every possible effort has been made to ensure that the information contained in this book is accurate at the time of going to press, and the publisher and author cannot accept responsibility for any errors or omissions, however caused. No responsibility for loss or damage occasioned to any person acting, or refraining from action, as a result of the material in this publication can be accepted by the editor, the publisher or the author.

First published in Great Britain and the United States in 2020 by Kogan Page Limited

Apart from any fair dealing for the purposes of research or private study, or criticism or review, as permitted under the Copyright, Designs and Patents Act 1988, this publication may only be reproduced, stored or transmitted, in any form or by any means, with the prior permission in writing of the publishers, or in the case of reprographic reproduction in accordance with the terms and licences issued by the CLA. Enquiries concerning reproduction outside these terms should be sent to the publishers at the undermentioned addresses:

2nd Floor, 45 Gee Street	122 W 27th St, 10th Floor	4737/23 Ansari Road
London	New York, NY 10001	Daryaganj
EC1V 3RS	USA	New Delhi 110002
United Kingdom		India
www.koganpage.com		

Kogan Page books are printed on paper from sustainable forests.

© Rob Baker, 2020

The right of Rob Baker to be identified as the author of this work has been asserted by him in accordance with the Copyright, Designs and Patents Act 1988.

ISBNs
Hardback   978 1 78966 296 2
Paperback   978 1 78966 294 8
eBook   978 1 78966 295 5

British Library Cataloguing-in-Publication Data

A CIP record for this book is available from the British Library.

Library of Congress Cataloging-in-Publication Data

Cataloging-in-Publication Data is available. Library of Congress Control Number: 2019055960

Typeset by Integra Software Services, Pondicherry
Print production managed by Jellyfish
Printed and bound by CPI Group (UK) Ltd, Croydon CR0 4YY

CONTENTS

ABOUT THE AUTHOR

Rob is a specialist in bringing positive psychology to work. He is the founder and Chief Positive Deviant of Tailored Thinking, a leading evidence-based positive psychology, wellbeing and HR consultancy.

Rob is world-leading when it comes to bringing job crafting to life within organizations. His work, ideas and research on how people can personalize work and bring their whole and best selves to the workplace have been presented at academic and professional conferences around the globe.

As a senior leader and consultant, Rob has delivered sector-leading and award-winning people initiatives and business transformation projects with organizations such as PwC and the University of Sheffield. Rob draws inspiration from helping others to find meaning, purpose and performance in their work.

Rob is a Chartered Fellow of the CIPD and a Chartered Fellow of the Australian HR Institute. He has a first-class Master's in Applied Positive Psychology from the University of Melbourne and continues to collaborate with academics from the University's Centre of Positive Psychology.

An avid runner, Rob has previously competed on the international stage, having represented Great Britain in mountain running and orienteering. These days, Rob runs and cycles purely for fun and reflection and enjoys outdoor misadventures with his family in Durham.

FOREWORD

The practitioner perspective

Andrew Dodman, Chief Human Resources Officer,
Leeds City Council

As Human Resources practitioners and leaders we instinctively appreciate that good work, innovative ways of working and great people management will profoundly affect an organization's ability to flourish and adapt to contextual change. We are also proud of the role that HR directly contributes to an organization's ability to successfully manage and lead its people. So why is it that our profession, our efforts and hard work are not always recognized as business critical? When explaining to people that I work in HR, why has it been the case that the response is: 'HR – that stands for Hardly Relevant doesn't it?'. Perhaps this is more a reflection on me than the wider HR profession, but I can't help wondering whether Rob Baker, in his first book, has identified an underpinning challenge to the HR and business community.

Whilst we readily recognize the causal relationship between good people management and business outcomes, it is perhaps the manner in which we apply our craft that lets us down. When attempting to deliver sound people management we almost always do it 'to' people; we tell them the policy and the procedure, we give the advice, guidance and decisions, we even prescribe the values and behaviours that each individual should hold whilst working, and the culture demanded across the workplace. Not all organizations are of course so standardized and regularized and many increasingly espouse the value of employee voice, engagement and experience. However, even within these progressive and enlightened workplaces, it is still HR that do the asking of the (staff survey) questions, analyse the answers and moreover take the affirmative management action to augment employee commitment and performance. At the heart of Rob Baker's book is a rather different paradigm, an approach that challenges the belief that HR management should be done to the workforce. In the alternative, he argues that each individual should be able to people manage themselves – to craft their own work, their own tasks, their own relationships, their own wellbeing, their own skills and their own career.

The approach is conceptually very simple to appreciate – crafting your own job will enable and encourage each person to bring their diverse, whole and best selves to work each day and as such foster engagement and performance. It argues that an organization's competitive advantage will ultimately come from the ability to exploit each employee's latent talent, and job crafting offers a mechanism to play to personal strengths and expose untapped potential. At its heart this book argues for the power of the individual. Instinctively we know this makes sense, for when we reflect back on our happiest and most productive periods within the workplace, we invariably consider individuals – maybe our line manager, a colleague or even ourselves. And we do so through the lens of being inspired by that individual and their unique creativity, thinking, behaviour and actions. Likewise, the single biggest complaint I receive from staff is when an HR intervention feels off-the-peg, entirely anodyne and ignores the needs and wants of the individual.

Rob Baker rightly argues that people strive for customization, choice and personalization. This book coherently argues that personalization at work, through job crafting, is not just another employee engagement tool or technique. Indeed it has much to say on the benefits it brings right across the whole array of HR interventions, whether in the areas of managing change, flexible working, health and wellbeing, performance management, diversity and inclusion or talent management. It is perhaps therefore surprising that a conceptually simple approach, and one that contributes so widely, is not at the forefront of every HR practitioner's current agenda.

Is this because job crafting is merely the latest fad and fashion, and therefore nothing more than a minor distraction to busy HR practitioners and leaders? Rob Baker tackles this head on and presents the empirical evidence base for personalization in work. The book also stresses that job crafting is not, by design, a monolithic top-down management or HR initiative that we brand and aggressively promote across our organizations. We see from numerous examples how job crafting is frequently applied discreetly, informally and tacitly. Its application could even be seen as everyday but is no less impactful to that individual who has chosen to craft their own job.

Has job crafting not permeated into HR practice because it presents a threat to management control? Could it compromise corporate structure, strategy, policy, procedure and well-established practice? Even worse could it diminish the size and scope of the HR practitioner! Again, Rob Baker carefully reflects upon this, arguing that job crafting is not a panacea but rather should relate and embed across the whole employment lifecycle.

Interestingly it is also argued that, within the current context of constant change and ambiguity, it is folly to expect decision making to rest solely with a small minority – managers and leaders. Organizations will only be able to adapt, create and innovate if all of their individual employees are able and willing to utilize their diverse talents.

The book provides many practical suggestions to help develop and promote job crafting. It encourages HR practitioners to play a key role in co-designing personalization principles whilst developing a supportive approach and culture to enable and trust people to 'safely' craft. Be warned though – HR should guard against owning job crafting and applying it systemically down the line. It is ultimately for each individual to consider what, where, why and when they should adapt and craft their job roles. So how should an HR practitioner start to consider this emerging and important human-centred approach to organizational management? It's obvious really. Start with the individual…with you! Have a go at crafting your own role, and through the practical support provided in this text, embrace your personal creativity, energy and commitment and let them reverberate around your organization.

FOREWORD
The academic perspective

Jane E Dutton, Robert L Kahn Distinguished University Professor Emerita, Ross School of Business, University of Michigan

Job design research has had a rich history born from applications of a job engineering approach applied to the improvement of jobs. The approach has been mostly top down, giving management and leadership the favoured position for knowing how, when and why to alter jobs so that they are performed in a more effective and fulfilling manner. Over the last 20 years this view of how to effectively design jobs has radically changed through the introduction of the idea of job crafting. Job crafting centre stages how employees themselves can make small changes to jobs that enable engagement, wellbeing and higher performance. This shift in perspective on how to approach the redesign of jobs has profound implications for how to improve and transform the possibilities for work, for human resource management and organizational science more broadly. Thankfully Rob Baker identifies and integrates 20 years of research on this process to make the case for why job crafting is important, how it fits the broader trend of personalization of work, and guides us in how to bring its practice and its power into any organization.

Sometimes forces converge and the time is just right for a book that integrates both academic research and practical interventions. This integration creates a useful and foundational guide for improving the way work is done and the difference it can make to individuals and organizations. Job crafting is a process and an approach to the design of work whose time has come. As Rob Baker effectively argues, it is an approach to work and human resource practice that fits beautifully the emphasis on personalization – but this time applied to the personalization of work as opposed to the personalization of products or services. At the same time, job crafting enhances creativity and innovativeness at work through small job changes that unleash human resourcefulness. Job crafting can be an engine for developing and reskilling talent as employees gain freedom and a capacity for improving the way that work is conducted in a direction that better develops and aligns with their strengths, interests and values. Research on the impacts of job crafting affirms that these assertions are more than abstract hopes, but are concrete results that deployers of job crafting can expect.

Besides these logical and compelling reasons for the timeliness of a practical book on job crafting, I wonder if the origins or research roots of the job crafting idea also contribute to the book's (and the concept's) appeal. In the late 1990s, Amy Wrzesniewski, Gelaye Debebe and I were a small research team endeavouring to explain how employees coped with devalued work. We interviewed a small group (23 to be exact) of cleaning support staff working at a local university hospital to learn from them about their everyday experience of doing this form of cleaning in a context where cleaning was obviously very critical to the organization's work. We were deeply inspired by a substantial number of the cleaners' accounts which detailed the small changes that these employees made in the conduct of their work that allowed them to care for the patients, the patients' families, the nurses and, sometimes, the doctors. This study was the origin and inspiration for the job crafting concept and the identification of different job crafting types. The fact that the cleaner examples are so often mentioned in accounts of job crafting (despite the unique and small sample study) makes me think there was something deeply humanizing and hopeful about the nature of work that was unearthed through this study and which has helped to propel its relative popularity. Job crafting as a concept and the hospital cleaners as living examples are testimonies to the generative possibilities of work as a site of human agency, creativity and engagement. These possibilities are waiting to be noticed and fostered if we adopt a more generous and developmental perspective on what people want to do and can do at work.

My hope is that all readers of *Personalization at Work* will be motivated to pursue the possibilities that arise from a more considered and systemic approach to job crafting. This book provides grounded and practical ideas for how to introduce, evaluate and improve approaches to job crafting, and useful examples of how various leaders and organizations have capitalized on this powerful job approach. It is an approach to fostering human flourishing at work that creates valuable and sustainable benefits while not requiring financial investment. However, job crafting as a form of personalization does require believing that this form of human enterprise at work is a meaningful and powerful way to unlock human potential at work. For me, this is a belief that I can stand by.

PREFACE

Why do some organizations and teams flourish whilst others flounder? What are the building blocks which enable exceptional performance from employees? How do people find genuine meaning and purpose in their work?

These are all questions that I have been constantly curious about throughout my HR career. And through formal study and personal research into the fields of positive psychology, behavioural science, HR and management I've endeavoured to explore and understand the extent of our knowledge from a scientific and academic perspective. It turns out we know a tremendous amount.

As an HR leader what I found particularly surprising is that this research isn't always widely known, shared or implemented in practice. This vast knowledge has largely remained unread and unexplored by HR and people professionals.

Job crafting, which is the central focus of this book, is an example of a concept that has been heavily researched from an academic perspective, but for a variety of reasons – which we will cover in this book – has been arguably untapped and under-translated into organizational practice. Job crafting describes people making changes to how they act, interact and think about their jobs to make them more personal. It invites, enables and encourages people to bring their diverse, whole and best selves to work each day.

The motivation for this book is to present the evidence for job crafting specifically, and a personalized approach to work more broadly, and blend this with practical ideas and case studies about how to bring this concept to life as an individual, in teams and across organizations. Of course, job crafting is not a panacea and its limitations and potential side-effects will be explored together with factors which can either amplify or inhibit a more tailored approach to work.

This book is structured into four different parts:

1 Explore
2 Experiment
3 Encourage
4 Embed

These parts represent the journey from learning about a concept to infusing it within and across an organization. In the exploration chapters, I will provide an introduction to why personalization at work matters and how people can personalize their work through the concept of job crafting. The experimentation part will give you an understanding of how you can personally explore job crafting within your own role and test it within your teams. The third part, Encourage, will provide ideas and research about how to enable and give energy to the concept of job crafting and highlight limitations and barriers. Lastly, the fourth part, Embed, will present an overview of how you can sustainably embed a job crafting mindset across an organization.

Whilst of course I have made every effort to avoid them, I've no doubt that there will be mistakes and errors in this book. These are mine, and mine alone. Similarly, whilst this book reflects my thinking and interpretation of evidence and research at the time of writing, I have no doubt that – and will in fact be disappointed if – my thinking doesn't evolve, change and develop in the future.

When reading this I actively encourage you to be curious and critical in appraising and evaluating the evidence, case studies and examples provided. I strongly believe in the ideas, concepts and research that I'm sharing with you in these pages, but I recognize that sitting alongside strong belief is potential bias. All I can say to you is that I am aware of this and have tried to be as balanced as possible in the information and details that I have shared.

I have had a number of conversations with researchers, academics and practitioners about the amount of detail and information to provide within the book. I am extremely conscious of diluting complex and nuanced ideas or cherry-picking results and outcomes from complicated studies. At the same time, I want this book to be readable, practical and assessable for curious but busy HR and people leaders. Getting this balance right in terms of depth and breadth of research and case studies has felt like a bit of a tightrope walk. Forgive me if I have wobbled at times in this text.

Some other things to be aware of

You will note that the spelling in this book is UK Oxford spelling which tends to use -ize rather than -ise in words such as personalize. To my ignorance, I found out that this is actually older in British English than the -ise form.

This book contains a number of examples and case studies. These are all based on specific examples that I have encountered through my work and my research. To help with clarity, conciseness, flow and in some cases confidentiality, the context of some of these examples has been changed slightly, as have individual names.

How to use this book

In the same way as I want you to make your work your own, please use this book in the way that best meets your personal needs. Whilst the book has been structured and designed to be read concurrently, I absolutely encourage you to skip sections and dive into others that are more relevant and interesting. In the same spirit, I promise I won't be offended if you scribble and scrawl throughout the book. Highlight away.

A measure of success for me – and you can let me know if you feel I've met this – is that you, the reader, feel confident and clear on what job crafting is and how it aligns to your individual ambitions and those of your organization. It would be fantastic if, having read *Personalization at Work*, you have the courage and curiosity to personally and proactively shape your own approach to work to make it more aligned to your strengths, passions and expertise. Let me know how you get on. Happy crafting.

ACKNOWLEDGEMENTS

I have been fantastically fortunate in my life to receive help, support and encouragement from many inspiring, interesting and caring people.

Firstly, I'd like to acknowledge the love and support from my wonderful family. To my wife Clare I'd like to say thank you for being you. You keep me inspired, sane, supported, grounded and loved. And continually asking myself 'so what?' Fin and Evie, your unconditional love is an unending source of energy and motivation. I hope that you will be able to create and craft your lives in ways that allow you to follow your dreams. To Mum and Dad, quite simply thank you for everything; your love, encouragement and gentle cheerleading means and has meant the world. To unCol, thanks for keeping me grounded. And keep up the advice.

Secondly, I would like to thank all the academics and researchers whose work and ideas have shaped my thinking. I have referenced and cited many of your great studies. Without your continued curiosity and investigation into how to make the world of work better this book would not have been possible – I'm standing on your shoulders. Specifically, I'd like to thank Gavin Slemp, Peggy Kern, Uta Bindl and Maggie Van den Heuvel for your willingness to collaborate and so generously and patiently sharing your wonderful wisdom and research.

The Centre of Positive Psychology at the University of Melbourne was instrumental in introducing me to many of the ideas and concepts which are the foundation of this book and I am so grateful to Lea Waters, Dianne Vella-Brodrick and Therese Joyce for giving me the encouragement and courage to apply the concepts and ideas I learnt about at the Centre in the 'real' world of work.

In terms of the book itself, I'd like to firstly like to thank the wonderful, wise and indefatigable Perry Timms for the unconditional personal encouragement and advice you have given me. Thank you to Alison Jones for helping to develop my half-thoughts into a (semi) coherent book outline. At Kogan Page, I'd like to thank everyone who has helped me, and specifically Lucy Carter for getting excited about and championing the book idea and Stephen Dunnell for the careful and cool way that you steered me through the writing process. A special thank you to Ian Miller (thanks cuz) for your design skills and Jessica Candy, Evan Jones and Katie Jones for your 'cover consultancy' support.

I've been tremendously lucky to have met many wonderful people through my work and research who have, knowingly or not, helped to shape, develop, challenge and change my thinking. People who have made a positive dent in my job crafting universe include: Alexandra Johnston, Andy Dodman, Anne-Marie Lister, Ash Buchanan, Belén Varela, Bob Merberg, Cecilie Torset, Charlie Leventon, Charlotte Axon, Chris Furnell, Claire Le Grice, Claire Walton, Duncan Archer, Elise Morris, Eva Maria Schielein, Gary Butterfield, Gary Turner, Geof Ellingham, Gethin Nadin, Gill Tait, Giselle Timmerman, Hannah Weisman, Heather Monro, James McGlynn, James Rutherford, Jessica Amortegui, Jo Fisher, Jo Murray, Jodie Lowe, John Turner, Jules Smith, Katie Leeman, Keith Peel, Lasse Kvarsnes Hansen, Lindi Teate, Lisa Davidson, Lorraine Masters, Lucy Harwood, Mandy Barker, Mark Crabtree, Mark Gilroy, Melanie Cheung, Melissa Beckett, Michael Hopkins, Michaela Schoberova, Michele Deeks, Michelle McQuaid, Michelle Minnikin, Naomi Woods, Natasha Wallace, Natal Dank, Nicola Leyden, Oenone Serle, Pamela Nuñez del Prado, Rachel Taylor, Richard Cooper, Rob Briner, Robert Ritchie, Sarah Cox, Sarah Dewar, Sharon Parker, Siv Heidi Breivik, Therese Joyce, Tracy Wray and Vikki Barnes. Thank you one and all.

To my family, past and present,
for your encouragement, love and support

PART ONE

Explore

01

Why personalization matters

Work is broken. If our work was an item of clothing, for most of us it would be a straitjacket. Or at best an ill-fitting suit. Modern working practices are failing us – constraining rather than amplifying our diverse skills, strengths, passions and interests. No wonder globally over 86 per cent[1,2] of us aren't fully engaged, excited and energized about our jobs.

As a society, and in business, people embrace opportunities for the personalization of products and services. We enjoy and value having our own individual style, beliefs and passions reflected in the things we do and how we do them. What if we encouraged people to customize their work the way a tailor would the final fit of a semi-tailored suit? What if we started to shape work around people rather than expecting people to constantly contort themselves around their jobs? What if we took a more personalized approach? What would an exceptional personalized people experience look and feel like? These are the questions that we will be exploring in this book.

So how can we bring a personal touch to our work? The answer lies in job crafting. Job crafting enables and encourages people to bring their diverse, whole and best selves to work each day in ways that foster engagement, job satisfaction, resilience and thriving. Job crafting is a research-informed and evidence-based approach to personalizing work and the research into this practice is compelling – it boosts innovation, nurtures health and wellbeing and amplifies meaning, purpose and productivity. This book focuses on what job crafting is, the positive impact it can have on individuals, teams and organizations, and how to practically encourage and embed a personalized people experience. But before diving into job crafting research, evidence and case studies, it's useful to explore the concept of personalization itself, why it matters and why it is missing from most organizations. This will be the focus for the first two chapters of this book.

In this first chapter, we will consider what personalization means, how different industries and sectors are evolving to enable and encourage greater customization, and why the ability to customize and shape objects and experiences makes us feel good and perform well. By exploring examples of how personalization is being used to create exceptional customer experiences we'll see what's possible with technology and creativity. By contrast, these illustrations will start to demonstrate how starkly an employee-centred and, arguably, human-centred mindset, is missing from the people experience in most workplaces.

The personalization revolution – a (very) brief history

Personalization is the action of designing or producing something to meet someone's individual requirements. Today, personalization permeates almost all aspects of our everyday lives, with the exception of most workplaces. We can now personalize our cars, our clothes and our holidays. This was not always the case. In the past, customization was the Rolls Royce or Savile Row of services, with the price tag to match. With new technology, production and information systems, costs are reducing and the benefits of personalization are more affordable and widely available. Reduction in costs combined with developments in digital technology has led to more enabled and interested consumers becoming engaged in customizing the products and services they buy.

'Off the shelf' is beginning to sound like an outdated and substandard term. As a society and in business, people enjoy and value having their own individual style, beliefs and passions reflected in what they do and how they do it. Consequently, consumers increasingly want products and services personalized and customized to meet and amplify their preferences, personalities and lifestyles.

Personalization is now all around us, but it is hard to pinpoint exactly when the concept moved from something that was a specialist luxury offering, to something more mainstream. One way to spot trends is to look at the use of a word or phrase in our modern language. Between 1950 and 2009, there was a 16-fold increase in the incidence of the terms 'personalisation' (the common British spelling) and 'personalization' (the Oxford English and American spelling) within the millions of books and articles that are scanned as part of the Google Books project.[3] Whilst the available data currently stops in 2009, as we will explore further in this chapter, there is nothing to indicate that the use of these words would have slowed down. In fact, there is everything to suggest that their use would have exploded further as opportunities to personalize our goods, services and lives in general have become both more accessible and affordable.

One-size doesn't fit all – insights from car manufacturing

In the past, car manufacturers and designers approached heterogeneity and diversity amongst their customers as a problem or business challenge to overcome. Over time this mindset has shifted and manufacturers are increasingly recognizing that responding to and tapping into individual preferences is a source of competitive advantage.

One of the most famous quotes made by Henry Ford, the founder of the Ford Motor company is: 'Any customer can have a car painted any colour that he wants so long as it is black'.[4] Ford made this comment in relation to the Model T car in 1909. Despite lobbying from his sales and design team, Ford was adamant that his company should save costs and leverage efficiencies by only offering one type of chassis and one colour of car. And that colour was black. In his autobiography,[5] Ford stated that his rationale was that 95 per cent of potential car purchasers were not interested in the colour of their car and that they should be focusing on these consumers rather than the 5 per cent – labelled by Ford as the 'special customers' – who were potentially interested in a more distinctive look. There is no denying that Ford's approach was successful; when the final Model T ran off the production line on 25 May 1927, over 15 million cars had been produced.

Whilst it is difficult to challenge the success of Ford's original thinking, it's certainly fair to say that the one-size-fits-all approach is not shared by modern car manufacturers and does not remain within the Ford Motor Company today. Today, all car buyers appear to want to be part of the 'special' 5 per cent that Henry Ford referred to and want to be able to customize and choose the specifications of their vehicles. As John Cooper, Vice President Customer Service Division at Ford Asia Pacific, said: 'Customers today view vehicles as an extension of their own personalities and are keen to customize their cars to stand out from the clutter.'[6] Modern car consumers are now able to personalize their vehicles with specifications way beyond the colour and the engine.

People who want a wider range of purchasing and personalization options are no longer thought of as demanding. To encourage and enable people to choose the options for their cars, Ford, along with other manufacturers, now have vehicle personalization centres across the world. These showrooms are set up to create a customized car-buying and driving experience. As well as being able to see and drive test and show cars, some showrooms now offer people the opportunity to use immersive technology to configure their cars. Having put on a virtual reality (VR) headset, customers of Volkswagen, Audi and Toyota are now able to see, feel and hear what their final car will look like.[7] Using augmented reality (AR) it's now possible for customers to use their smartphone or tablet to project what their car will look like sitting on the driveway of their house.

From mass production to mass customization

In the same way that mass production and standardized production are key legacies of the first Industrial Revolution, mass customization and personalization can be indelibly linked to today's technological revolution, which is fuelled by digital advancements in artificial intelligence, machine learning and robotics. From a production perspective, mass customization enables products to be manufactured at scale that can be individually customized and tailored to the specifications of the purchaser. The distinctive aspect of mass customization is that the customer is a critical and integral part of the design process and is in effect a co-designer of the final product. Whilst modern technology is now enabling mass customization at scale, it is not an entirely new idea. The first modern description of mass customization can be traced[8] to the American futurist and writer Alvin Toffler and his 1971 book *Future Shock*,[9] which described a new paradigm in manufacturing where personalized products and services could be provided to consumers with efficiency and at scale.

Digital development and the internet revolution have enabled organizations to connect the manufacturing or service technologies with the consumer in a cost-effective and high-quality way. The internet provided a platform for organizations to launch online configurators, which enabled customers to customize elements of the products they were purchasing. One of the earliest and best-known companies to do this was Nike. NikeID (now known as Nike by You), allows customers to personalize elements of their footwear such as colours and include personal messages and motifs to be stitched on. Today, rather than only being able to personalize an existing design, 3D printing and other manufacturing technologies allow consumers to easily upload and print one-of-a-kind products. Websites such as Ponoko and Zazzle, for example, allow customers to create personalized gifts and items using 3D printing technology.

Positive disruption through personalization

The movement towards personalization, choice and customization is disrupting how industries and sectors are operating. As Professor Frank Piller, co-founder of the MIT Smart Customization Group, states:[10]

> Mass customization means to profit from the fact that all people are different. Many managers regard heterogeneity of demand as a threat, as a challenge to overcome. I see it, however, as an extraordinary profit opportunity. If you set up the right processes and product architectures, you can serve your customers individually and efficiently at the same time. Exactly this is the essence of mass customization.

Through his research, Professor Piller, together with his colleagues and collaborators, argues that mass customization has the potential to benefit both the business and the customers.[11] Consumers are able to purchase personalized goods and services that meet with, and match, their needs and preferences at a price point they are willing to pay, and businesses are able to profit from this service. As we will explore in later chapters, there is a similar benefit for organizations and employees in the creation of a personalized workplace; people get to work in ways that best fit their personal styles and strengths and organizations benefit from the additional performance, engagement and discretionary effort that this way of working provides.

Some examples of personalization in practice

To get a sense of just how much personalization is now a part of everyday lives, it is useful to consider examples of how the ability to shape our products around us as individuals is fundamentally shaking up the way we shop for, and consume, our clothes, cars, food and medicines.

CARS
In 2018 Mini launched the Mini Yours customized range. Described as 'the next stage of personalization', Mini offers customers the opportunity to be the designer of their own, 'one-of-a-kind' Mini. This enables drivers to literally put their signature on their car. Through an online portal, and using 3D print and laser-cutting technology, consumers are able to produce personalized items such as dashboards with individualized pictures or names. Using special lights hidden underneath the car's wing mirrors, the car is able to

project a custom message or image onto the pavement when you unlock the car or open the door.

MEDICINE

Our health is shaped by our genetic make-up combined with environmental and lifestyle factors. In the past, so-called 'blockbuster'[12] medicines were developed to treat as broad a range of people as possible. Using the traditional treatment approach, almost all patients with the same condition would receive the same drug, even though in reality it may only have been 30–60 per cent effective across the population. To get a medical licence, pharmaceutical companies would need to prove that it was safe to use amongst the whole population. This took time and was tremendously costly.

Personalized medicines revolutionized the treatment process. Through the combination of analysis of information about our genomes with clinical and diagnostic data it is now possible to identify our risk of susceptibility to ailments and disease and to develop potential treatments to stop them. Building on these insights gained from genomic and diagnostic analysis, different subtypes of individuals who suffer with the same condition can be identified and treatment can be developed and ultimately tailored to target the underlying cause.

The treatment of cancers is one area where this approach is increasingly commonplace in, for example, the NHS in the UK. As all cancers have a genetic basis, it is possible to develop a genetic or molecular diagnosis which can be used to identify the most effective treatment. This approach has been found to significantly improve the chance of survival, compared with traditional 'broad' diagnosis and treatment.

PERSONALIZED FOOD AND NUTRITION

DNA testing is not only being used to provide personalized healthcare. Personalized nutrition services have been around since 2016, led by Habit in the United States. Nestlé launched a similar service in 2018, which it is piloting in Japan.[13] These services typically send new customers a testing kit consisting of a swab to collect your saliva and a fingerprick test to collect a small sample of blood. This enables your DNA profile to be analysed. Depending on the service you are using, your genetic profile can be developed for up to 60 different biomarkers, identifying deficiencies in key minerals, vitamins and hormones and tolerance levels and sensitivities. In response to this analysis, customers are sent a customized dietary and nutrition report outlining how their body reacts to different food groups. In order to work with, rather than against, their biological profile and life-style goals, customers are able to buy personalized recipes, meal kits or ready-made meals.

PERSONALIZED CLOTHING

Most clothing purchases could be described as 'off the peg' – customers select from pre-made items in store, or online, which best fit their personal size and sense of style. For many of us, working with a stylist or getting tailor-fitted clothing is a once-in-a-lifetime occurrence saved for weddings or significant life events when we want to look and feel our best. Increasingly clothing manufacturers and retailers are looking to find ways to disrupt and challenge the existing way we buy clothes and create more opportunities to have clothes made or sourced based on individual specifications.

Zozo and Stitch Fix are two examples of companies that have put person-alization and personal style into the heart of clothes buying. Stitch Fix, founded by Katrina Lake in 2011, has the mission to 'change the way people find clothes by combining technology with the personal touch of experi-enced style experts'.[14] For a small fee Stitch Fix asks people to complete a style survey online and then through a combination of algorithms and human stylists the company curates a selection of items which it sends to customers. Delivery and returns are free. The company went public in the United States in 2017 with a valuation of $1.4 billion.[15] An arguably more ambitious, but certainly less successful clothing business is Zozo. The Japanese company's ambition was to produce bespoke clothing on a mass scale. In order to collect measurements, Zozo sent a skintight 'Zozosuit' to people's homes. Each suit had more than 350 white dots which were scanned using a special smartphone app. Once a customer's unique measurements had been collected they were able to order bespoke clothing including t-shirts, blouses, trousers and dresses. This idea appears to have been ahead of its time and in April 2019 Zozo discontinued services outside of Japan.[16] There are, however, a number of organizations betting on a personalized revolution in clothing and, perhaps most notably, Amazon currently holds a patent for an 'on demand' customized clothing manufacturing system.[17]

Why personalization matters

Why do we value personalization and why is it important? These are two questions that we will explore in this next section, with help and insights from TV shows on Netflix and the experience of building flat-pack furniture from IKEA.

Personalization sparks joy

Intuitively many of us understand that we tend to value and appreciate the things we build and create. To get a sense of this you only need to watch an episode of *Tidying Up with Marie Kondo* on Netflix. Marie is an organizing consultant and author. In her hit TV show she works with people to declutter and organize their lives by focusing on the items that they store, use and display in their homes. To practise the Kondo method, people are instructed to sort through the items in their house one by one, keeping only those that 'spark joy' and discarding those that don't.

On the show, when people sort through their household objects, the items that people cling on to tend to be things people have created, customized or have a personal story attached to them. The 'keep items' that spark joy tend to be personally constructed or built furniture, jewellery, clothing, photos or correspondence which have sentimental and personal resonance. To the viewer it is sometimes surprising to see what people want to hold onto – some of the 'keep' items do not look especially beautiful or aesthetically pleasing – but it is clear that to the participants these items are precious. If there is a theme it is that they tend to reflect something personal about that participant, trigger a memory or story, or represent a chapter in that person's life.

The IKEA effect

Through a series of ingenious experiments, scientists have been able to explore why, when it comes to personalization, beauty really is in the eye of the beholder. Or to put it another way, why we value the things we build.

Researchers Michael Norton at the Harvard Business School, Daniel Mochon from the University of California and San Diego, and Dan Ariely at Duke University were curious about whether physically constructing an item influenced people's perceptions of its value. In their initial study they randomly assigned participants as 'builders' or 'inspectors'. Builders were asked to assemble a plain black cardboard box from IKEA using standard instructions. Inspectors were given a ready-made box and had the opportunity to examine it.[18]

At the end of the study, participants were in possession of identical boxes. The only difference being that half the group had played a part in putting the box together. Before the study finished, participants were asked to place a bid on the box. They were also asked to rate how much they liked the box. Builders bid significantly (over 1.5 times) more than inspectors and their ratings of how much they liked the box were higher too. The researchers coined the term the 'IKEA effect' to refer to the phenomenon of people placing additional value on items that they have played a part in constructing compared with ready-built goods and services.

Although the Norton *et al* study was relatively modest in size, the IKEA effect has been found to be present in a number of subsequent and preceding studies involving items such as origami, LEGO[19] and even lottery tickets.[20] In the case of the origami experiment, participants were willing to pay almost the same for their poorly constructed beginner's effort (in this case a frog) compared with the same aesthetically perfect animal constructed by an origami expert.

Consistently, people attach greater value to the things that they build than if someone else built the very same product. Intuitively, the IKEA effect makes sense. We may all have experienced an attachment to, or affection for, a self-assembled item of furniture. This is often even more surprising because – and particularly in my case – they tend to be poorly constructed. A personal example of this is the filing cabinets in my office which I restored and painted. When I moved offices, I was able to make use of some old cabinets that a business in Durham was getting rid of. I had to take the cabinets apart and put them back together again. I sanded them down and repainted them. The time it took to do this cost much more than it would have been to buy cabinets from new. And if I'm honest I did a pretty terrible job. But I now love these cabinets, even though they stick and you need to be careful not to rub the paint off when you walk past. The reason I have an affection for the cabinets is that in a small way they are part of me – they reflect my personal taste in the colour they are painted, my belief in hard work in having to put them together, and my commitment to recycling and limiting waste.

KEY PERSONALIZATION PRINCIPLES

When working with businesses to explore their work design and people experience, I suggest that leaders consider three principles when it comes to personalization in the workplace:

> **Principle 1:** People (may) like what you give to them.
>
> **Principle 2:** If you want people to value something let them build it.
>
> **Principle 3:** If you want people to love something then let them create and shape it.

Enhancing performance through personalization

As well as influencing the extent to which we like and value an object, personalization can provide us with a performance advantage. This is particularly the case with objects that allow people to self-express through the customization process. In a study published in the American Marketing Academy's *Journal of Marketing*, Ulrike Kaiser and Martin Schreier from Vienna University of Economics and Business, and Chris Janiszewski of the University of Miami Research, investigated the link between personalization and performance.[21]

In the first stage of the experiment participants were asked to either select or design a pen which they were told would be used to advertise the university where the study was being carried out. Two weeks later the participants returned to collect their pen and whilst they were there were asked to complete some additional tasks. This including a challenge to generate as many two- to eight-letter words from the letters D, S, E, T, N, R, I. The length of time people spent on the exercise (their motivation) was recorded, together with the number of correct words produced (performance). Participants who completed the task using a pen they had designed themselves spent over 23 per cent longer on the task compared with those using a standard 'off the shelf' pen they had previously selected. And those using a self-designed pen were more accurate too. They were nearly 18 per cent more accurate. The research team went on to find similar results with exercises using personalized versus standardized beer mats (the exercise involved flipping) and dart flights (the task involved hitting targets with a dart).

Why personalization influences performance

Researchers provide a number of potential reasons why personalization appears to increase motivation and by extension performance. First, the customization process transfers the individual's identity to the end product. Customization extends a part of the self into the product and, in effect, makes the product an extension of the self. Consequently, a person has stronger attachment to the product, and is more committed, willing and motivated to use the product to achieve the goals or tasks that they are pursuing. An interesting conclusion from this research is that there appears to be an advantage in allowing self-expression in the tasks that we do. The golden shoes worn by Usain Bolt at the 2016 Olympics look like a shrewd investment (and a nice marketing ploy too I'm sure) and may explain the trend for football stars to personalize their boots.

The psychology of personalization

Whilst the pull towards personalization may feel natural, researchers from the fields of psychology, marketing and economics continue to explore the reasons that we are drawn to objects, products and services that have been shaped and built by us. Broadly four factors either explain or directly influence why we value personalization:

- preference fit;
- accomplishment;
- investment of effort;
- origination.

Preference fit

Preference fit refers to the match between a person's preferences and a specific product or service. You can think about this as whether or not an item reflects our personal taste and style. Not surprisingly, people tend to value items that have a strong preference fit (a match between their personal style and the item) more highly compared to products where there is a weaker match.

Understanding people's preference fit matters because if someone ultimately doesn't like the style or make-up of a final product they are going to value it less than someone who feels that it has a strong match. Most of us can relate to this, when we have given a fake smile or an insincere thank you for a present we have received that we know we will never use because it does not match our personal tastes. At work, the equivalent is being given a task or asked to be involved in a project that either we don't enjoy (there is not a good match to our skills and strengths) or we don't see or value its purpose (there is not a good fit between our values and beliefs).

Preference fit can also explain why we do sometimes value the things we have played no part in designing. Most of the objects or experiences we buy are not customized or personalized. This does not mean we won't enjoy them, but it is contingent on our tastes and preferences. Similarly, at work, being told a decision doesn't mean we won't value or respect it, but if we have no part in contributing to it, then the extent to which we may be motivated by the decision will be contingent on whether or not it matches our personal beliefs and values.

Accomplishment

Fundamentally, as humans, we value opportunities to demonstrate to ourselves and others that we can successfully achieve and accomplish things. We tend to get satisfaction from doing and creating things. You can see it in the eyes of children when they have finished their latest LEGO project and why a beer or glass of wine in the evening tastes so good after having spent the day gardening or working through thorny life administration tasks. Psychologists argue that accomplishment feeds our need to show competency and efficacy, which is deeply embedded in our human nature.[22] By building something, people are able to control and shape elements of their environment and in doing so are also able to demonstrate competence to themselves and others in terms of what they have created. Building our own stuff ultimately amplifies our feelings of passion, pride and competence.

If you inhibit or take away people's sense of accomplishment from an item they have constructed then you can also impact on people's affinity and value. Researchers ingeniously tested this through a LEGO building task.[23] Participants were split into two groups and both were asked to build identical models. At the end of the experiment, one group were asked to dismantle the models, whilst the other group kept the model intact. Both groups were then asked to value the models. The dismantlers valued the model significantly less than those whose models remained intact; effectively, the researchers had taken away the former group's feelings of accomplishment.

Effort

Economists have known for some time that the more effort and energy people put into the pursuit of something, the more they tend to value it. So a partial explanation of the power of personalization is that the effort invested in the customization or personalization process transfers, or rubs off, onto the product and leads to an overall greater attachment. This might explain why home-grown fruit and vegetables are often thought to taste better. The secret to the superior taste might not just be down to freshness, but could also be explained by the 'effort effect'. The fact that we have toiled in the growing process means that we are ultimately going to value the end product more than something we bought off the shelf at the local supermarket. The effort effect exists in other animals too. Research with other animals including rats[24] and pigeons[25] have shown a preference for sources of food that have required an effort to obtain.

Origination

People tend to value items where they feel they have been the creator or originator. By shaping, crafting or creating an object, people's personal fingerprints are figuratively and sometimes literally on the final product or outcome. In laboratory experiments, marketing researchers Nikolaus Franke, Martin Schreier and Ulrike Kaiser found that people valued self-designed artefacts simply because they felt that they were the originators of the object. They referred to this as the 'I designed it myself' effect. Through a series of studies involving items such as scarfs, wristwatches, t-shirts and skis they consistently found that participants gave a higher valuation to items which they had been able to create or design themselves compared with objects that were similar, but not identical, in style that had no, or limited, options to customize.[26] The study found that the effect is even stronger when the customization factor is rated as enjoyable and when the customer or participant feels that they have contributed most to the final outcome.

Origination of a product also enables people to reflect their personal identity. In an interview in the *New Scientist*,[27] Kelly Herd, a marketing researcher from Indiana University, highlighted that personalizing a product provides an opportunity to show a person's true self. She argued that this tapped into a fundamental human need and explains why people will pay more for items that they have personalized or customized themselves. As she puts it, 'People create pretty objectively unattractive stuff but they love it.'

Interaction of personalization factors

Whilst each of these pillars of personalization impacts on people's feelings of value, it is important to recognize that they can each interact with and influence each other. For example, researchers have demonstrated[28] that whilst the effort and energy involved in the personalization process are linked to augmented levels of value, this is only the case when people value the final product (eg there is a strong preference fit). If the end product has a low subjective preference fit – then the effort and energy involved in the creation are seen as a cost rather than an investment and this ultimately has a negative impact on the value of the product. At the extreme level, this could be illustrated by an artist destroying the canvas of an artwork that they have been toiling on, or a child, in a fit of rage and frustration, pulling apart a LEGO model they have been building if it doesn't look like they had imagined it would.

Conclusion

There are clear reasons which explain why customer-focused organizations are increasingly creating opportunities for consumers to customize and individualize the products, services and experiences they can buy. A sense that we have actively contributed to the creation of an item makes us feel a greater affinity and attachment to that product. We value it more than something we have simply been given. Personalized goods not only feel better; in the right circumstances they let us perform better too.

The ability to personalize the products and services around us extends to almost all aspects of our lives. There is, however, one significant area of our lives where a tailored and human-centred approach is often missing: the workplace. Despite the potential benefits in terms of profits and performance, few organizations are embracing a personalized approach to work. From a technological perspective we are now in what many are calling the fourth Industrial Revolution, but our leadership styles and management practices still seem tethered to management ideas that are over 120 years old. The reason for, and the cost of, the stubborn persistence of traditional 'top down', 'control heavy' and 'mass production' working practices and leadership styles will be the focus of the next chapter.

KEY POINTS

- We are going through a personalization revolution in all aspects of our lives – with the exception of the way we work.

- People tend to value the things they build and love the things that they create and personalize.

- Personalization can give us a performance advantage as it fuels motivation and lets us express ourselves positively.

- The power of personalization can be explained by four factors: preference fit, accomplishment, investment of effort, and origination.

KEY QUESTIONS

- What do you see as the key benefits of personalization?

- What opportunities are there for people to personalize their jobs and work in your organization?

- To what extent do you encourage people to be part of a key decision and change processes within your organization?

Notes

1 Gallup State of the Global Workplace report, available from: https://www.gallup.com/workplace/238079/state-global-workplace-2017. aspx?utm_source=2013StateofGlobalWorkplaceReport&utm_medium=2013S OGWReportLandingPage&utm_campaign=2013StateofGlobalReport_ Redirectto2017page&utm_content=download2017now_textlink (archived at https://perma.cc/9XR5-59FU)

2 ADP Global Study of Engagement, available from: https://www.adp.com/-/ media/adp/resourcehub/pdf/adpri/adpri0100_2018_engagement_executive_ summary_release%20ready.ashx (archived at https://perma.cc/PN5K-CYNP)

3 Michel, J B, Shen, Y K, Aiden, A P, Veres, A, Gray, M K, Pickett, J P, Hoiberg, D, Clancy, D, Norvig, P, Orwant, J and Pinker, S (2011) Quantitative analysis of culture using millions of digitized books, *Science*, **331** (6014), pp 176–82

4 Ford, H and Crowther, S (1922) *My Life and Work: In collaboration with Samuel Crowther*, Cornstalk Publishing Company

5   Ibid
6   Ford (2015) Ford goes further in enhancing ownership experience; launches industry-first vehicle personalisation centre in India, available from: https://www.india.ford.com/about-ford/media/newsroom/2015/feb-5/ (archived at https://perma.cc/P6UC-W3Y9)
7   Zerolight, Projects and references, available from: https://zerolight.com/projects#all-projects (archived at https://perma.cc/S64D-ZEW9)
8   Jiao, J, Ma, Q and Tseng, M M (2003) Towards high value-added products and services: mass customization and beyond, *Technovation*, **23** (10), pp 809–21
9   Toffler, Alvin (1971) *Future Shock*, New York, Bantam Books
10 Piller, F (nd) Mass customization, available from: http://frankpiller.com/mass-customization/ (archived at https://perma.cc/SPW9-GD4G)
11 Salvador, F, De Holan, P M and Piller, F (2009) Cracking the code of mass customization, *MIT Sloan Management Review*, **50** (3), pp 71–78
12 NHS England (2016) Improving outcomes through personalized medicine, available at: https://www.england.nhs.uk/wp-content/uploads/2016/09/improving-outcomes-personalised-medicine.pdf (archived at https://perma.cc/8BPC-PTNV)
13 Purdy, C (2018) Nestlé is using DNA to create personalized diets in Japan, *Quartz*, available at: https://qz.com/1376737/nestle-nesn-nsrgy-is-using-dna-to-create-personalized-diets/ (archived at https://perma.cc/3PF9-842U)
14 https://www.stitchfix.co.uk/about (archived at https://perma.cc/9F6N-RN5U)
15 Salmon, F (2019) The rise and fall of Stitchfix, *Axios*, available at: https://www.axios.com/stitch-fix-ipo-valuation-d7897131-5585-41dc-9c73-e87867ce169a.html (archived at https://perma.cc/VB8S-VT7L)
16 Bain, M (2019) Zozo's grand experiment in cheap, customized clothing was ahead of its time, *Quartzy*, available at: https://qz.com/quartzy/1605585/zozo-cancels-plan-to-sell-cheap-custom-clothes-internationally/ (archived at https://perma.cc/R2EA-7SWM)
17 Wingfield, N and Couturier, K (2017) Detailing Amazon's custom-clothing patent, *New York Times*, available at: https://www.nytimes.com/2017/04/30/technology/detailing-amazons-custom-clothing-patent.html (archived at https://perma.cc/4ZR5-4KTF)
18 Mochon, D, Norton, M I and Ariely, D (2012) Bolstering and restoring feelings of competence via the IKEA effect, *International Journal of Research in Marketing*, **29** (4), pp 363–69
19 Ibid
20 Risen, J L and Gilovich, T (2007) Another look at why people are reluctant to exchange lottery tickets, *Journal of Personality and Social Psychology*, **93** (1), p 12
21 Kaiser, U, Schreier, M and Janiszewski, C (2017) The self-expressive customization of a product can improve performance, *Journal of Marketing Research*, **54** (5), pp 816–31

22 Franke, N, Schreier, M and Kaiser, U (2010) The 'I designed it myself' effect in mass customization, *Management Science*, **56** (1), pp 125–40, available at: http://www.jstor.org/stable/27784096 (archived at https://perma.cc/6E5P-AY6A)

23 Mochon, D, Norton, M I and Ariely, D (2012) (see note 18 above)

24 Lydall, E S, Gilmour, G and Dwyer, DM (2010) Rats place greater value on rewards produced by high effort: an animal analogue of the 'effort justification' effect, *Journal of Experimental Social Psychology*, **46** (6), pp 1134–37

25 Friedrich, A M and Zentall, T R (2004) Pigeons shift their preference toward locations of food that take more effort to obtain, *Behavioural Processes*, **67** (3), pp 405–15

26 Franke, N, Schreier, M and Kaiser, U (2010) The 'I designed it myself' effect in mass customization, *Management Science*, **56** (1), pp 125–40

27 Spinney, L (2011) The hard way: our odd desire to do it ourselves, *New Scientist*, available at: https://www.newscientist.com/article/mg21228441-800-the-hard-way-our-odd-desire-to-do-it-ourselves/#ixzz648nYuChR (archived at https://perma.cc/NP8H-5PUT)

28 Franke, N and Schreier, M (2010) Why customers value self-designed products: the importance of process effort and enjoyment, *Journal of Product Innovation Management*, **27** (7), pp 1020–31

02

Why personalization is missing from our work

At the start of the Industrial Revolution, as people moved to cities to work in newly established factories, there was at first little consistency in the way work was assigned, structured and carried out. It was largely trial and error, with one factory operating differently from another. There was no clear understanding of the best way to structure work or indeed what output was possible or achievable. That was until the arrival of Frederick Winslow Taylor in the early 1900s. Standing on the shoulders of Adam Smith, who first introduced the idea of division of labour, Taylor had very clear ideas about the best way to organize and structure work. His answer was a more scientific approach to management and it's fair to say that discretion, empowerment and engagement were not at the top of his list.

The Principles of Scientific Management written by Taylor and published in 1911[1] was arguably the first management book blockbuster and included clear prescriptions on how work should be structured and organized. The best way to boost productivity according to Taylor was to simplify complex jobs into individual tasks, measure everything that workers do and link performance and pay by giving incentives and bonuses to high performers and punishing and ultimately sacking those who failed to make the grade. Taylor stipulated that jobs were engineered to ensure that unnecessary work was eliminated and that the most efficient work methods in terms of production for each task were investigated, identified and then standardized for all workers undertaking the same activity. It required breaking work down into the smallest possible components.

Taylor was fastidious about understanding the minutiae of tasks and the optimum timing and exact spacing of rest breaks during the working day for maximum efficiency. Taylor's detailed approach is perhaps best illustrated in his study of the Bethlehem Steel Works in 1898.[2] Through various trials he found that the optimum scoop and load for a worker to shovel should be 21 pounds (9.5 kilograms). This was the goldilocks weight; it was not too heavy to prematurely tire the worker out, but also not so light as to allow for any slacking. During the study, and I'm sure to his horror, he found that workers were using the same types of spade irrespective of the type of material they were shovelling. Those moving lighter material such as ash would have a much smaller load than 21 pounds, and those shovelling iron ore would have a much heavier challenge. In response, Taylor developed eight different specialized blade sizes to work with different densities of materials. This led to a reported daily output growth from 16 to 59 tonnes per shovel.

Taylor proposed that manual workers should undertake the physical labour of the role, and that managers and supervisors were focused on undertaking the thinking and cognitive elements of the work. The implication of this was that supervisors made all the decisions with little or no input or recognition of the thoughts of the workers themselves. In fact, the key role for supervisors (or bosses, as Taylor referred to them) was to ensure total compliance and no deviation from the prescribed approach; supervisors were stationed by workers at all times. Any problems in terms of poor performance were dealt with by a specialist supervisor with the title 'disciplinarian'.

To provide motivation for employees, monetary bonuses were established and paid upon the successful completion of work, provided that workers precisely followed the scientific and detailed instructions they had been given. This bonus was the quite literal compensation for giving up the freedom in the way they carried out their work.

Scientific management became popular because it provided the holy grail of low labour costs and high production output. It also made recruitment easier. Finding and replacing people was straightforward. The production methods were so tightly controlled that there was little training or experience required.

Does any of this sound familiar? Are any alarm bells starting to ring? They should be. As the world around us is undergoing a personalization revolution, work design and leadership styles have gone largely untouched. Increasingly organizations are embedding and embracing personalization in their external customer experience but it is often missing from their internal people experience. Whilst manufacturing, production and service offerings have continually evolved and transformed, our approach to management and working practice has not kept pace. If anything, for many of us the way that work is structured and managed shows the long tail of the first Industrial Revolution. This chapter will explore why standardized and controlling management practices and work design still exist, and look at the key drivers for change from individual, organizational and societal perspectives.

The long tail of scientific management

The legacy of industrial engineering or scientific management is very much alive in many of our working practices today. In 2018 Amazon patented designs for wristbands which precisely track where workers are placing their hands. The bands send vibration signals to steer the workers to inventory bins, making the fulfilment process more time efficient.[3] The movement to a gig economy is in effect an outsourced model of piecemeal working, where pay is contingent on completing individual tasks in set ways. In 2019, Hermes announced that delivery drivers would be entitled to more favourable contracts, offering entitlements such as holiday pay, but only in return for a commitment to follow the precise driving instructions stipulated by the company.[4] This is no progress at all from the compensation practices offered by Taylor to incentivize or control workers in the 1900s.

Beyond distribution or logistics, many of us will be familiar with a style of management that favours control and compliance rather than commitment and consent. In these workplaces decisions are often made for, not with, people and performance targets are set by senior managers with little or no discussion with the people actually doing the work.

A further way to spot the legacy of Taylorism is in the way organizations are structured, represented in the humble organizational chart. Diagrams that show leaders at the top and workers at the bottom have hardly evolved since the 1800s. The font used and the printing quality might have changed but the management thinking has not. As Aaron Dignan outlines in his book *Brave New Work*,[5] when he shares different organigrams with audiences they consistently struggle to differentiate between those developed in the 1800s and those produced in the present day. Organigrams represent where the power dynamic resides in businesses and it almost always flows from top to bottom. It is a physical representation of a mindset that senior leaders are the ones best placed to make decisions on behalf of others.

Why organizations rely on control and compliance

Arguably, the impact of Taylorism on management thinking is as profound and pervasive as the influence of Newton and Einstein on physics. The question of why this thinking has been so significant in imprinting itself over the last 120 years is unclear. First, it potentially stems from the belief that the role of the most senior leader or manager is to make key decisions, a phenomenon sometimes referred to as HIPPO (highest paid person's opinion), where the most senior person in a group is always the one with the final say. Second, it is easier to measure the external factors that go into work rather than the factors going on inside the human body. And with technology, monitoring and analysis are becoming increasingly easier. For example, it is now possible to record and analyse the content of every conversation and interaction between colleagues using smart name tags[6] or monitor the progress of building work on construction sites using drones.[7] Third, it's clear that control and command practices do work, at least in the short term with activities that have clear tasks and controllable outputs. In environments that have a focus on short-term profits and outcomes, it makes sense that leaders will fall back on tried-and-tested techniques they studied at business school or which are already baked into the DNA of their organization. Lastly, trying to minimize the idiosyncrasies of human behaviour through standardization and regularization will, on the face of it, lead to more stable and predictable outcomes. Humans are inherently messy in terms of their thinking and predictability and it is understandable that leaders will want to tamper this diversity down in the name of stability and possibly sanity.

The cost of control and compliance

Whilst there is no doubting that from some perspectives piecemeal production and top-down hierarchical structures appear to work in terms of short-term productivity, efficiency and output, they are not sustainable or desirable in the longer term. The tolls of undertaking repetitive tasks with low skill variety and an absence of autonomy have been known for as long as these work design practices have been used.

The first *Journal of Applied Psychology*, published in 1917, contains a number of articles detailing the challenges of controlling management practices. The librarian G G McChesney writes (p 176):[8]

The human interest element in industry may be a new phrase, but it is certainly a crying need in the industrial world to-day.

Is there no inspiration in labor? Must the man who goes on forever in a deadly routine, fall into the habit of mechanical nothingness, and reap the reward of only so much drudgery and so much pay? I think not.

McChesney highlights a key failing of scientific management, which is that it does not acknowledge or recognize the humanity of the people doing the work. Effectively, the scientific approach treats people as cogs in a machine. Any and all control or variance in how work is done is stripped out. Squeezing autonomy out of work may produce short-term benefits but has tremendous costs in terms of sickness, turnover, rebellion and reputation and employee brand over the longer term.

Writing in the same 1917 journal, E H Fish, an employment manager in the Norton Company in Worcester Massachusetts, highlights that organizations using Taylorism principles had average turnover rates of less than a year. His interpretation, which appears to be supported by others with an interest in work psychology at the time, is that Taylorism was making work unsustainable and that as a consequence people were forced to leave their work, or they were being sacked as a result of their inability to meet quotas and targets. To illustrate the cost of this turnover, E H Fish writes (p 162):[9]

There are approximately 40,000,000 working people in the United States and nearly 50,000,000 changes in work each year each of which calls for a considerable expenditure in training for the new job. The cost in wages lost, in spoiled work, in time of foreman or instructor consumed, ranges from less than ten dollars in the case of a laborer to a thousand dollars or more for men in executive positions. If we assume the average cost of changing jobs to be $25, which is surely conservative, the loss to the country is a round billion dollars each year.

It is of course now more widely recognized amongst HR and people professionals that turnover has direct and indirect costs to organizations and the colleagues around them. The limitations and damage of a controlling approach to management have been in plain sight almost since the inception and foundation of the ideas themselves and the contributions and thoughts of Mr McChesney and Mr Fish show that we have known about these problems for over 100 years. Despite this knowledge, controlling and top-down management practices remain part of the fabric of business practice. Today, there is more data than ever before to support the notion that people don't enjoy or feel fully engaged in their work. Before we turn our attention to this data, we will explore other factors which explain why people don't personalize work.

Why people don't personalize their work

If Taylorism or controlling leadership styles explain why personalization at work is restricted from a top-down perspective, on the face of it, there is nothing to stop workers themselves from trying to make small shifts to personalize their work to make it better. The truth is that many people simply run out of energy or motivation to be proactive in how they engage with their work. Or worse still, they potentially never had this interest or enthusiasm in the first place. Whilst there are many possible factors that may explain this, two appear to be particularly prevalent: learned helplessness and a desire to conform.

Learned helplessness

A potential legacy of a controlling work environment is learned helplessness. The foundation for this concept came from literally shocking experiments with animals, most infamously dogs. One of the first experiments into learned helplessness by Martin Seligman from the University of Pennsylvania and Steven Maier from the University of Colorado would most likely horrify ethics approval boards today. Their study demonstrated that dogs who had been exposed to inescapable and unavoidable electric shocks in a previous experiment failed to avoid shocks in future tests, even when escape was possible.[10]

Seligman and Maier's experiment had two stages. For the first part of the study dogs were placed into one of three groups. Dogs in group one were strapped into harnesses and not given any shocks. Group two were put into harnesses (delightfully named as a Pavlovian hammock) and given intermittent electric shocks which they could stop by pressing a panel with their noses. The dogs in group three were isolated but paired with group two dogs and received the same intensity and duration of shocks as the second group. This third group of dogs had no ability to stop or control the shocks.

For the second part of the experiment the dogs were placed in a box divided into compartments with a short, easy-to-jump partition between the two. The first compartment was electrified and gave intermittent shocks. When placed in the electrified compartment, dogs from groups one and two quickly learnt that they could avoid shocks by jumping to the other side of the box. Those in the third group – the ones who had previously received no control over their shocks – took no such action. They were observed to sit still quietly, whining until the shocks terminated.

Seligman used the term 'learned helplessness' to describe this third group. The dogs' initial experience of being unable to escape or control their environment had created a mindset that meant that they felt unable or unwilling to change or positively alter their circumstances. As Seligman writes (p 407):[11]

> Uncontrollable events can significantly debilitate organisms: they produce passivity in the face of trauma, inability to learn that responding is effective, and emotional stress in animals, and possibly, depression in man.

Whilst we are unlikely to receive shocks at work – at least of the electrical kind – in my experience working with organizations, many people show learned helplessness. You may have witnessed signs of people feeling unable or unwilling to change their circumstances amongst people you have worked with. These colleagues appear to be unwilling or unmotivated to try to shape their work, or they will tell you that an idea or solution you suggest will never work and is doomed to failure based on their previous experiences.

Bad experiences which we have no control over negatively influence our motivation, our ability to think rationally and our emotional states. After a series of these types of experiences people will – understandably – shut down both emotionally and motivationally. Our personal resilience and tolerance levels in being able to buffer against negative experiences may differ, but over time even engaged, happy and hardworking people can face burnout and stress in the face of persistent negative experiences with no hope or ability to positively influence their circumstances. For example, an employee in a new job may try to develop their role or innovate how work is done. If these attempts are continually thwarted, or even worse, punished by colleagues or senior managers, they will eventually cease to even try. Any desire and motivation to innovate will have been squeezed out of them.

A desire to conform

Humans have a natural desire to conform and cooperate – it has helped us evolve, develop and survive as a species. Whilst a drive to 'fit in' with others may have been useful from an evolutionary perspective, it doesn't always serve us, or organizations, well in the modern workplace. Conformity at work can be seen in many different ways: through the nature of our interactions, the way people express emotions, how decisions are made, the support provided to colleagues and even the clothes we wear. Whilst modest amounts of conformity are useful for social cohesion and coordination, a compulsion to behave, act and think like the others around us can have a number of negative consequences.

In an article for the *Harvard Business Review* entitled 'Let your workers rebel', Professor Francesca Gino from the Harvard Business School outlined the prevalence of conformity in the workplace.[12] A survey by Professor Gino of over 2,000 US employees from a variety of sectors revealed that over half of people working in companies she had recently surveyed felt compelled and encouraged to conform and a similar number stated that, culturally, people across the organization never challenged or questioned the status quo. Organizations that actively embrace a diversity of ideas are in the minority. In a separate study of over 1,000 employees, Professor Gino reports that less than 10 per cent of people stated that they worked in organizations that actively embraced and encouraged non-conformity.[13] From these surveys at least, a large number of people felt that they were unable to bring their individual self to the workplace and instead were encouraged to bring a different identity or mask to work.

People often conform because they want to fit in with the group (known as normative influence) and because they may ultimately believe that the group is more knowledgeable or better informed. But there is a downside: such behaviour can quickly lead to 'group think' or a lack of creativity and diversity of ideas. From the outside, it may be easy to spot this type of behaviour in action. If you are in a group it can be often difficult to break outside of these existing norms. Humans often see the potential losses of challenging social conventions and behaviours as being more significant than the potential benefits or gains from rebelling or challenging the status quo.

Whilst there are a number of reasons why we might go along with the consensus, there are consequences of doing so, particularly if you don't fully agree or align with decisions being made or how others are behaving. For the individual, Professor Gino argues that conforming often creates dissonance which collides and contradicts with our true individual preferences and ultimately can make us feel inauthentic. This explains why doing work you don't believe to be morally right, or letting inappropriate behaviour, such as a sexist remark, go unchallenged feels so wrong. Gino's research with colleagues[14] has found that experiencing or remembering situations of inauthenticity, compared with authenticity, consistently led to participants feeling immoral and impure and wanting to literally clean themselves and take more positive and pro-social behaviour such as helping others or donating money.

At an organizational level, the consequences of cultures that encourage conformity can be debilitating. Organizations that create environments that crush the individuality out of individuals don't benefit from the diversity of thinking, strengths and perspectives that sit – often untapped – within their workforce. A failure to allow people to contribute as individuals can, at best, lead to boredom and, at worst, result in complacency and inertia. At an organizational level it can lead to corporate stagnation where businesses fail to innovate and grow.

Why we need personalization at work

There are many reasons from an individual, organizational and societal perspective that we should be embracing the heterogeneity that makes us unique and human. The next section will explore eight key drivers for a personalized and tailored approach to work from distinct but often overlapping perspectives. These are:

- low levels of enjoyment and engagement;
- worryingly low levels of wellbeing;
- our work defines us;
- we can't be our true selves at work;
- we are sleep-working;
- we're all wired differently;
- purpose and meaning are missing;
- an uncertain future.

Low levels of enjoyment and engagement

Many, in fact the vast majority of us, aren't engaged in or don't enjoy the work that we do. To illustrate this point, I often start presentations with a slide using autocomplete suggestions generated that day from the Google search bar. When we use Google search, algorithms predict what we are going to type based on previous searches. Today, as I write this, the top autocomplete suggestions when I type 'My job is...' are:

making me depressed

boring

making me ill

too stressful

too hard

pointless

killing my soul

done here

ruining my life

For those looking for more empirical data, Gallup is probably the most well-known and cited report on employee engagement and satisfaction at work. Aggregate data collected by Gallup in 2014, 2015 and 2016 across 155 countries reported in the 2017 State of the Global Workplace Report[15] indicates that just 15 per cent of employees worldwide are engaged in their work. Gallup's definition for engagement is employees who are highly involved in and energized about their work. Two-thirds of respondents state they are not engaged and don't feel a sense of attachment to their work or workplace. Finally, 18 per cent are what Gallup refers to as actively disengaged. These individuals are described as being psychologically unattached to their work and the company they work for.

The data available from European and UK workplace and skill surveys also shows a troubling trend of increased job demands and diminishing resources. The European Working Conditions Survey showed that between 2010 and 2015 there was a small, but significant, increase in the proportion of people stating that their job involved working at a very high speed all or most of the time.[16] A similar trend has been seen in the UK through the Skills and Employment Survey (SES),[17] a national representative survey of individuals that has collected data from working adults across the UK. A comparison of SES shows that levels of work intensity and job demands have continually increased since 1992. Worryingly, task discretion has moved in the opposite direction. And job control – reflected by the extent to which people can shape their work – has also sharply decreased.[18]

You may be reading this thinking that the Gallup or workplace survey results don't reflect the feedback you collect through your engagement or pulse survey scores. Don't pat yourself on the back too quickly. Management and organizational scholars have shown that whilst people may look or even report to be engaged, at a service level, in reality the picture is more nuanced and complex. Research by Dr Amy Armstrong and her team at Ashridge-Hult Executive Education[19] found that only a quarter of teams who were originally identified as highly engaged using an internal survey were found to be fully energized and engaged by their work when observed in practice. Almost a third (32 per cent) were actually actively disengaged and 14 per cent were merely satisfied. The remaining 29 per cent of teams were found to be 'pseudo-engaged'. This term was used to describe those teams which appeared to be highly engaged on the surface but in reality, following careful observation, were found to be dysfunctional.

Worryingly low levels of wellbeing

Over 600,000 people in the UK suffer from work-related stress, resulting in an estimated 12.5 million working days lost each year.[20] The 2017 American Psychological Association publication 'Stress in America' reported that work was one of three highest sources of reported stress – along with money and concerns about the future of the nation. The consequences of workplace stress are estimated to cost the US healthcare system as much as $200 billion a year, with a corresponding cost to employers of over $300 billion annually in employee turnover and lost productivity.[21] The most chronic form of workplace stress is burnout, described in the World Health Organization's International Classification of Disease as a 'state of vital exhaustion'.[22] The wellbeing of our workplaces is unlikely to improve any time soon. The 2019 CIPD Health and Well-Being report highlighted that nearly two-fifths of 1,078 people professionals from companies in the UK have seen an increase in stress-related absence over the last year.[23]

An inability to personalize or shape work could partially explain the negative levels of wellbeing, stress and health that are being reported. Our ability to control our work directly affects mental health and physical health outcomes. A cross-sectional study of hospital employees across Europe has found that in Western Europe there was a positive relationship between job autonomy and physical and mental health.[24] More shockingly, in his book *Dying for a Paycheck*,[25] Professor Jeffrey Pfeffer highlights a longitudinal study from Indiana University which found that people in jobs with high job demands but low levels of job control had a 15.4 per cent higher mortality rate.

Our work now defines us

Never before has so much of our identity and self-worth been tied up to our work. Work has moved beyond something that we have to do, to something that defines us as individuals. You only have to think about the last party or event you went to. How quickly did you ask, or did someone ask you, 'What do you do?' It didn't take very long I would wager. This question gives us something to talk about but also gives us an insight into that person's world.

This sense of importance of work was captured in a 2015 YouGov survey conducted for the Recruitment & Employment Confederation[26] where members of the UK public were given a list of 10 life decisions that people generally have to make and asked them to select options that they rated as 'important'. The most popular answer was 'what to do as a job'. Over three-quarters of people (77 per cent) rated this as the most significant lifetime decision. This is even more stark when you compare the other important decisions that respondents were asked about, including 'when to start a family' (73 per cent), 'where to live' (64 per cent), 'whether to get married (or enter into a civil partnership)' (57 per cent) and 'who their friends are' (37 per cent).

We can't be our true selves at work

Writers and philosophers from Sartre to Socrates have recognized our need as humans to show others our true selves, yet this form of self-expression is rarely, if at all, encouraged or enabled at work. This is despite consistent and compelling research which has shown that when people are able to tap into and use their strengths, and express themselves fully in their jobs, they are more engaged and energized. And they perform better too.

In his book *Alive at Work*,[27] Professor of Organizational Behaviour Dan Cable outlines that as humans it is part of our biology to seek out activities that are motivating and enable us to explore our individual strengths and to find opportunities for personal growth and stimulation. As Professor Cable explained to me: 'There's something hard-wired into us that wants to have a unique identity and fulfil our unique potential. If we are able to do this, it lights us up as human beings – it creates and sustains enthusiasm and energy.' And business leaders should care about this because as Professor Cable describes, 'this energy and creativity gets ploughed right back into our work'.

Studies of the brain have found that when what neuroscientists call our 'seeking systems' are stimulated, we get rewarded with a dose of dopamine, which is a neurotransmitter linked to both motivation and pleasure. Switched-on seeking systems make us feel more motivated, purposeful and ultimately alive. Unfortunately, for many of us, our work is shutting down these systems in our brains as we are starved of opportunities for play, experimentation, exploration and learning.

Professor Cable believes that enabling people to personalize their work experiences is one way to access our seeking systems and encourage people to awaken the potential lying dormant in workplaces across the world. He explains:

> By allowing people to adapt their work you allow the incumbent job holder to be energized in exceptional ways, meaning what they're putting into the job is not ordinary, but is extraordinary. It's fundamentally a different level of zest, energy, creativity and curiosity, encapsulated in a profound feeling that 'this job allows me to be my best'.

An inability to use and apply our unique talents and strengths in the workplace is another way in which people are often prevented from bringing their full selves to work. In an article for the *Harvard Business Review*,[28] Brandon Rigoni and Jim Asplund from the Gallup Institute highlighted research which demonstrated a strong correlation between strength use and performance. Their findings were drawn from 49,495 business units with 1.2 million employees across 22 organizations in seven industries and 45 countries. The number of hours each day that people stated they were able to use their personal strengths was positively linked to those individuals reporting 'being energetic', 'learning something interesting', 'being happy' and 'smiling and laughing a lot'. Additionally, people who used their strengths every day were more than three times more likely to report having an excellent quality of life and over six times more likely to be engaged at work.

We are sleep-working

Without realizing it we spend much of our working day on automatic pilot. We are sleep-working through our tasks. Many of us will walk into the office, switch on the computer and find ourselves half-way through a mountain of emails before we know it. We often give little thought to how or what we want to achieve that day. When we sleep-work, it feels like someone else is in control of the day.

There's good reason for our autopilot. The average adult makes around 35,000 decisions each day.[29] Our brains have evolved unconscious decision-making processes to enable us to make basic decisions and perform routine tasks and activities with little mental effort or energy. This mechanism is there to protect us from reaching mental overload. But as with a number of our neurological evolutions there are unintended consequences. Whilst unconscious decision-making capacities might protect us from overloading they also have the capacity to disengage us from what we are doing.

The Nobel Award-winning behavioural economist Professor Daniel Kahneman offers some insight into how we process information around us. In his book *Thinking, Fast and Slow*,[30] he describes two different systems for thinking: System 1 and System 2. System 1 is our automatic pilot and thinking takes place primarily in the amygdala and other parts of our brain that developed early in our evolution. Our thinking using System 1 is automatic, rapid and unconscious; it happens without us knowing about it. Whilst it is ruthlessly energy efficient, making it ideal for making fast decisions with minimal information, it is not always as effective as we would like it to be and is susceptible to bias and error.

System 2 thinking is, by contrast, slow, deliberate and conscious. It happens with wilful attention and energy. It is typically more methodical and critical and therefore more reliable than System 1 thinking. System 2 thinking is useful when we need to undertake more rationale, complex and logical tasks. System 2's rational cognitive processes take place primarily around the prefrontal cortex and the elements of our brain that have evolved more recently.

We spend over 90 per cent of our time in System 1 thinking. Kahneman's research and work demonstrates that whilst we tend to think we are rational beings making clear decisions, the majority of our thinking is being done automatically and subconsciously.

So why does it matter that we are sleep-working and on autopilot during the day? There are certainly aspects of our work where our automatic pilot serves us well: navigating around the office, using software applications and performing routine tasks. But for those in roles which require critical thinking, creativity and analysis, working on autopilot is not useful. Our thinking is literally lazy and prone to bias and error.

In order to create a more personalized approach to our work, individuals need to be more deliberate in the way they approach and carry out their tasks and responsibilities. Customized working requires people to create the time, space and energy to think about their work in order to shape it accordingly. This also makes it more likely that people will spot the routines and habits at work that are potentially unhelpful and can be changed.

We're all wired differently

We have over 300 trillion neural connections in our heads, maybe more. Neuroscientists are showing how these connections are constantly shaping and evolving. It's an impossibility that any two people see and process the world in the exact same way.

Typically, managers don't recognize, and therefore make the most of, our diversity. At worst, managers ignore and even stifle our individual differences. Others with better intentions may try to engage with people the way that they themselves would like to be treated. This, despite what our parents may have told us, may not be the best advice. Making assumptions about people's preferences based on our own values and experiences fails to acknowledge and recognize the individual we are engaging with. We are all different. Just because you like something it doesn't mean that someone else will. For example, some people might like to receive praise as loudly and publicly as possible. Others can think of nothing worse than being at the centre of attention. For these individuals a discreet thank you email or note may be much more valued and appreciated.

Positive leaders and managers ask questions that enable them to learn about the people they support. They don't make assumptions or force their perspectives on others. Open, coaching-style questions can be useful in understanding the preferences and preferred styles of working of your colleagues. Similarly, fairness across an organization does not mean that everyone is treated as, and gets, the same. Instead, we should be exploring individual preferences and needs and striving to meet them. It is this consistency of approach rather than a dogged pursuit of fairness and equity that we should be striving for.

Purpose and meaning are missing

In 2020 millennials (those born between 1981 and 1996) are forecast to make up 35 per cent of the global workforce, and are poised to represent the majority of the UK's workforce by 2025.[31] They are, and will continue to be, a significant part of the working population and have been subject to a number of reports and studies of their make-up, mindset and motivations at work.

Consistently, factors that are reported as mattering most to millennials in terms of their work are that it:[32]

- has meaning and a wider purpose;
- enables personal growth and development;
- taps into individual strengths and passions.

Whilst these factors have been identified by millennials as being important to them, arguably, a desire for a more 'human-centred' approach to work is something that is universally valued by all, irrespective of age or generation.

In order to meet the explicit needs and expectations of their workforce, many organizations are going to have to change their approach to work design. A more personalized approach to work is likely to appeal to the millennial demographic as it recognizes and builds upon their individual talents and interests.

Research by Facebook has also shown the importance of having meaning and purpose in work.[33] Facebook's HR and People Growth team, working with people analytics, undertook analysis to understand why some people left Facebook and others stayed; they were surprised by the results.

Facebook found that meeting the personalized needs of their people was a better predictor of retention than people's relationship with their manager or colleagues. People weren't leaving because of bad bosses; they were leaving because of bad jobs. Further information collected and analysed by Facebook's data analytics team found that compared with people who left, those that stayed were more likely to report enjoyment at work, alignment to their strengths and opportunities for positive growth and progression. Specifically, workers who were staying at Facebook found work 31 per cent more enjoyable, used their strengths 33 per cent more often and expressed 37 per cent more confidence that they were growing the skills and experiences that were important to their careers compared with those who left.[34] Many people who left Facebook appeared to have found personalization, purpose and meaning were missing from their work. In response to these findings the HR and People Growth team have focused more on understanding individual passions and interests of their people and on encouraging them to find ways to craft and personalize their jobs.

The future is uncertain

At the World Economic Forum in Davos in 2018, the Canadian president Justin Trudeau gave a speech on future economic global challenges. At the heart of his speech was the need to adapt to and positively respond to change. In his public address to the forum,[35] he eloquently described the challenges businesses, leaders, policy makers and politicians are facing. He said:

The pace of change has never been this fast, yet it will never be this slow again.

In order to harness and move with, rather than getting swept away by, the waves of change, business leaders across the world will be increasingly required to develop strategies to meet the challenges and opportunities of change and innovation. This will include ensuring that people have the right blend of skills and expertise to do their work effectively, efficiently and enjoyably.

In the crystal ball-gazing game of predicting future work trends played by researchers, consultants and futurists, there is great debate about what impact technological advancement will ultimately have on how our work is done and which jobs will be needed. Predictions have ranged from Keynesian-tinged descriptions of widespread automation-driven disruption and unemployment and 'jobless futures' to more optimistic views of growth and the development of human-machine work. These hybrid 'super jobs' are predicted to be infused with artificial intelligence that focuses on performing transactional and routine elements of a job, resulting in more opportunities for more complex and non-standardized 'human' elements of work including collaboration, connection and creativity.

Similarly, core skills that organizations will need to develop, promote and sustain in the future are also innately human. The 'Future of Jobs Report 2018' from the Centre for the New Economy and Society[36] highlights the importance of 'human' skills in the future of work and specifically creativity, originality and initiative. Critical thinking, persuasion and negotiation are similarly expected to retain – or increase in – importance, along with qualities such as attention to detail, resilience, flexibility and complex problem solving. Emotional intelligence, the ability to influence and a service orientation are also all expected to have an increase in demand.

Whilst many predictions of the future of work differ starkly from each other, they all tend to be consistent in predicting considerable change and transformation in relation to how work is currently structured. This will require change to individual job roles and opportunities for people to learn new skills and ways of working. Traditional reactive, top-down and controlling management styles are unlikely to be agile enough to keep pace with the levels of innovation, continuous improvement and transformation needed. Approaches to working that cultivate creativity and commitment amongst workers and are flexible and adaptable are more likely to offer sustainable competitive advantage. As we will see throughout this book, evidence shows that personalized, individual and 'human centred' approaches are those more likely to create these types of behaviours and outcomes.

Conclusion

The best organizations, and the best managers, put people at the heart of their thinking. They find talented people and create jobs and work around them. But too often leaders don't know enough about what gives their colleagues energy and makes them feel truly alive at work. Employees often don't have their passions and priorities recognized or are not given opportunities to fully utilize their strengths. We are constraining rather than unleashing the talents and potential of the people who work for us. And as a consequence, our outdated approach to organizational design and management practices is sucking the life and energy from workplaces.

In the same way that climate change deniers refuse to acknowledge the irrefutable evidence to the contrary, many leaders in organizations fail to engage with the science that demonstrates that their approach to work design is causing harm to their employees and ultimately their bottom line. Disengagement, ill health and a lack of innovation and productivity are the organizational equivalent of melting ice sheets in Greenland and the Antarctic. But we can change this. We can catch up with the personalization revolution that is happening around all around us and create work that amplifies rather than tempers our talents and strengths. In order to engage and energize people in their work, 'human centred' approaches which offer meaning, growth and development are going to be more important than ever.

So how can we personalize our work? One answer, which we will explore in the next chapters, lies in the concept of job crafting. Job crafting is an approach that enables individuals and teams to actively shape and tailor their work around their passions, strengths and interests. It invites, enables and encourages people to bring their diverse, whole and best selves to work each day. Like people, job crafting comes in all different shapes and sizes.

KEY POINTS

- Scientific management focuses on carefully identifying and controlling the component parts of how work is done.

- Many leaders continue to adopt a leadership style centred on control and compliance which can be traced back to scientific management and the 1900s.

- People may be reluctant to personalize their work because of learned helplessness and an overall desire to conform with others and not disrupt the status quo.

- The way work is currently designed and delivered in most workplaces does not make the most of our individual talents, strengths and passions.

KEY QUESTIONS

- Do you see the legacy of Taylorism and scientific management in your workplace?
- To what extent do people in your organization feel empowered and encouraged to innovate and challenge conformity?
- Of the eight separate reasons given for why we need to personalize work, which ones do you feel are the most significant?

Notes

1 Taylor, FW (1911) *The Principles of Scientific Management*, New York, NY, USA and London, UK
2 Ibid
3 Solon, O (2018) Amazon patents wristband that tracks warehouse workers' movements, *Guardian*, available at: https://www.theguardian.com/technology/2018/jan/31/amazon-warehouse-wristband-tracking (archived at https://perma.cc/3KDL-GSU6)
4 BBC News (2019) Hermes in 'ground-breaking' deal for couriers, available from: https://www.bbc.co.uk/news/business-47110934 (archived at https://perma.cc/7XUK-WH3Q)
5 Dignan, A (2019) *Brave New Work: Are you ready to reinvent your organization?* Penguin UK
6 Bruno, M (nd) Smart badges: ready-to-wear networking, *EVENTTECHBRIEF*, available at: http://www.eventtechbrief.com/top-stories/smart-badges-ready-to-wear-networking (archived at https://perma.cc/F69D-SP54)
7 Spade Technology (nd) How drones are being used for imaging construction sites, available at: https://www.spadetechnology.com/how-drones-are-being-used-for-imaging-construction-sites/ (archived at https://perma.cc/Y8D4-QEVL)
8 McChesney, G G (1917) The psychology of efficiency, *Journal of Applied Psychology*, 1 (2), pp 176–79 http://dx.doi.org/10.1037/h0075424 (archived at https://perma.cc/7WEE-DAUH)
9 Fish, E H (1917) The psychology of efficiency, *Journal of Applied Psychology*, 1, 162–72 http://dx.doi.org/10.1037/h0075424 (archived at https://perma.cc/7WEE-DAUH)
10 Seligman, M E and Maier, S F (1967) Failure to escape traumatic shock, *Journal of Experimental Psychology*, 74 (1), p 1
11 Ibid

12 Gino, F (2016) Let your workers rebel, *Harvard Business Review*, Oct–Nov, available at: https://hbr.org/cover-story/2016/10/let-your-workers-rebel (archived at https://perma.cc/8SHC-HHD7)

13 Ibid

14 Gino, F, Kouchaki, M and Galinsky, A D (2015) The moral virtue of authenticity: how inauthenticity produces feelings of immorality and impurity, *Psychological Science*, **26** (7), pp 983–96

15 Gallup (2017) State of the global workplace report, available at: https://www.gallup.com/workplace/238079/state-global-workplace-2017.aspx?utm_source=2013StateofGlobalWorkplaceReport&utm_medium=2013SOGWReportLandingPage&utm_campaign=2013StateofGlobalReport_Redirectto2017page&utm_content=download2017now_textlink (archived at https://perma.cc/3QR6-J2HF)

16 Eurofound (2016), Sixth European Working Conditions Survey – Overview report, Publications Office of the European Union, Luxembourg

17 Green, F *et al* (2017) Work intensity in Britain, available at: https://www.cardiff.ac.uk/__data/assets/pdf_file/0009/1309455/4_Intensity_Minireport_Final.pdf (archived at https://perma.cc/T95Y-NKAL)

18 Gallie, D *et al* (2017) Participation at work in Britain: first findings from the skills and employment survey 2017, available at: https://www.cardiff.ac.uk/__data/assets/pdf_file/0010/1309456/5_Participation_Minireport_Final.pdf (archived at https://perma.cc/PJ25-VKD6)

19 Armstrong, A (2018) Do engagement surveys tell the whole story? *People Management*, available at: https://www.peoplemanagement.co.uk/voices/comment/do-engagement-surveys-tell-whole-story?utm_source=mc&utm_medium=email&utm_content=pm_daily_07122018.12/7/2018.673901.Opinion:+Do+engagement+surveys+tell+the+whole+story%3F&utm_campaign=&utm_term=1137615 (archived at https://perma.cc/FDF5-T2CR)

20 Health and Safety Executive (2019) Work-related stress, anxiety or depression statistics in Great Britain, 2019, available at: http://www.hse.gov.uk/statistics/causdis/stress.pdf (archived at https://perma.cc/UM3H-JWNK)

21 Pyrillis, R (2017) Employers missing the point of rising employee stress, *Workforce*, available at: https://www.workforce.com/2017/03/14/employers-missing-point-rising-employee-stress/ (archived at https://perma.cc/3DA3-T29E)

22 Burn-out (definition), available at: https://icd.who.int/browse10/2016/en#/Z73.0 (archived at https://perma.cc/SWW7-3A55)

23 CIPD (2018) Health and well-being at work, available at: https://www.cipd.co.uk/knowledge/culture/well-being/health-well-being-work (archived at https://perma.cc/Z788-Q5VV)

24 Faragher, E B, Cass, M and Cooper, C L (2005) The relationship between job satisfaction and health: a meta-analysis, *Occupational and Environmental Medicine*, **62** (2), pp 105–12

25 Pfeffer, J (2018) *Dying For a Paycheck: How modern management harms employee health and company performance – and what we can do about it*, HarperCollins

26 Skoulding, L (2018) How long does the average UK employee spend at work? *Accountancy Age*, available at: https://www.accountancyage.com/2018/10/02/how-long-does-the-average-uk-employee-spend-at-work/ (archived at https://perma.cc/5TGS-PPCA)

27 Cable, D (2018) *Alive at Work: The neuroscience of helping your people love what they do*, Harvard Business Review Press

28 Rigoni, B and Asplund, G (2016) Developing employees' strengths boosts sales, profit, and engagement, *Harvard Business Review*, 1 September, available at: https://hbr.org/2016/09/developing-employees-strengths-boosts-sales-profit-and-engagement (archived at https://perma.cc/P284-TEXB)

29 Hoomans, J (2015) 35,000 decisions: the great choices of strategic leaders, *Leading Edge Journal*, available at: https://go.roberts.edu/leadingedge/the-great-choices-of-strategic-leaders (archived at https://perma.cc/4F2E-CHGC)

30 Kahneman, D (2011) *Thinking, Fast and Slow*, Macmillan

31 Tilford, C (2018) The millennial moment – in charts, *Financial Times*, available at: https://www.ft.com/content/f81ac17a-68ae-11e8-b6eb-4acfcfb08c11 (archived at https://perma.cc/3C8R-VL8X)

32 Hershatter, A and Epstein, M (2010) Millennials and the world of work: An organization and management perspective, *Journal of Business and Psychology*, 25 (2), pp 211–22a

33 Goler, L *et al* (2018) Why people really quit their jobs, *Harvard Business Review*, 11 January, available at: https://hbr.org/2018/01/why-people-really-quit-their-jobs (archived at https://perma.cc/H3PP-LLXS)

34 Ibid

35 World Economic Forum (2018) Justin Trudeau's Davos address in full, available at: https://www.weforum.org/agenda/2018/01/pm-keynote-remarks-for-world-economic-forum-2018/ (archived at https://perma.cc/W83Q-2NL9)

36 World Economic Forum (2018) The Future of Jobs Report 2018, available at: http://www3.weforum.org/docs/WEF_Future_of_Jobs_2018.pdf (archived at https://perma.cc/9R64-6NR8)

03

An introduction to job crafting

Crafting a personalized approach to work

Job crafting enables people to proactively personalize their approach to work. Most people find that they have job crafted before without even realizing that they have done it. They are familiar with the notion of taking control and shifting aspects of their work in subtle ways that align more with their personal and professional needs, skills and interests, and also recognize the sense of satisfaction, control, enjoyment and confidence that this brings.

When I am introducing the concept to people for the first time, I often show them a picture I took from a popular men's clothing chain, which specializes in suits, shirts, shoes and jackets. I was browsing one day when I noticed a badge on the cuff of one of the suits. Just before I was accosted by a diligent security guard, I was able to take a picture of the badge, which I often share in presentations. The badge said 'Tailor me, to make me more you'. The badge was advertising the fact that the suit could be semi-tailored. The customer would be buying a standard suit and therefore would not be able to change the suit's core elements such as the colour and style but they could personalize the final fit based on their individual dimensions and specifications.

Job crafting is a semi-tailored approach to working. The basic design and structure of a job has been established but the final fit and how the job is undertaken is subtly shaped to reflect the strengths, passions and needs of the individual worker. The benefit of job crafting is that it enables people to create a closer fit between their work and their individual needs, motivations and circumstances. Similar to people who feel more comfortable and confident wearing clothing which reflects their personal style and physical shape, workers who job craft feel more satisfied, energized and engaged in their work. And they perform better too.

This chapter will provide an introduction to the concept of job crafting, and explore its origins from a research perspective with links to contemporary theories of work design and practice.

An introduction to job crafting

In the autumn of 2014, Google sponsored a one-day event which brought together 175 thinkers including world-leading academics and behavioural scientists, researchers, consultants, chief people officers and people leaders to re-envision work and the workplace.[1] The focus of the day, which was entitled re:Work, was to collaboratively explore ways that employers and employees could create meaning at work, how to make work better, and how to change the nature of work itself.

One of the invited speakers at the event was Amy Wrzesniewski, a Professor of Organization Behaviour at Yale School of Management. Professor Wrzesniewski gave a presentation on job crafting and described how she, together with colleagues Jane Dutton and Gelaye Debebe had first come across this approach to work.[2] Together, the researchers were studying the work of cleaners at a university hospital. Specifically, they were interested in how these individuals found meaning in their work, how they experienced work, what they enjoyed and what they found lacking. What the team uncovered astonished them and inspired further study, ultimately leading to a fundamentally new approach to work design.

As part of their initial study, the researchers talked to the cleaners about their personal perceptions and views about the work they did. Curiously, they found that the cleaners broadly fell into one of two groups. The first group described their work in exactly the way we might expect. They didn't feel that the work was highly skilled or satisfying and described their motivations for working being primarily financial. They were working for the pay cheque and nothing else. And when this group were asked about the tasks and activities involved in their work, they described the basic physical activities that you would expect a cleaner to undertake: mopping, cleaning, sterilizing.

The second group described their work completely differently. They enjoyed their work and found it deeply meaningful; they thought of their work as highly skilled. When the researchers explored with this second group the core tasks and key relationships, they described the work in very different terms. In fact, listening to them, you could have been fooled into thinking they had been doing completely different jobs. The types of activities they were doing included paying attention to which patients seemed upset so that they could double back and see them during their shift to give them an opportunity to talk or even cry. These cleaners described proactively finding opportunities to help other people, such as escorting members of a patient's family through the maze of corridors back to their cars in the carpark, which ensured that the patient didn't have to worry about them getting back safely. One of the cleaners interviewed who covered areas of the hospital where people were in, and recovering from, comas, described how they moved around pictures that hung on the patients' walls on a regular basis in order to provide a more stimulating environment. When the researchers probed further about whether this was part of her expected duties she replied, 'That's not part of my job but that's part of me'.[3] Another cleaner from this second, more engaged group, described her role as being an ambassador for the hospital. Others used the word 'healer' because they created clean and sterile spaces where patients could heal.

Working with her colleague Jane Dutton, Professor Wrzesniewski continued to research and investigate the differences between the two groups. They found that the distinction between how people valued and enjoyed their job was not down to how the job had been formally designed by managers, but how some of the cleaners were proactively shaping and changing the design of the work themselves. The difference wasn't top down and management-led; it was the opposite – bottom up and employee-led. They considered a number of different phrases to describe this behaviour including job architecturing, but ultimately, job crafting was the one that stuck.

Together with Professor Dutton and Assistant Professor Justin Berg, Professor Wrzesniewski went on to formally define job crafting as:

> Something employees do to redesign their own jobs from the bottom up in a way that fosters their engagement at work, their satisfaction at work, their resilience and their thriving.[4]

Job crafting involves people personalizing their approach to, and the delivery of, their work. It is not a trick of the mind involving people thinking differently about the work they do; it fundamentally leads to positive changes to how work is done, how they connect with others and the value and enjoyment they derive from their work.

Job crafting and work design

Job crafting is distinct from many job re-design approaches which are traditionally top-down and manager-led processes with no, or minimal, input from employees.[5] More traditional job design processes are often static and minimize opportunities for agility and flexibility. By contrast, job crafting is centred around the individual purposefully and proactively personalizing their work without the requirement for input from managers (see Figure 3.1). Job crafting is dynamic and based on the needs, motivations and preferences of the employee in response to the challenges and opportunities that they are facing. As we will explore in more detail in Chapter 9, job crafting and a bottom-up approach to job design can be used to embed a personalized people experience across an organization.

FIGURE 3.1 Job crafting, work design and job configuration

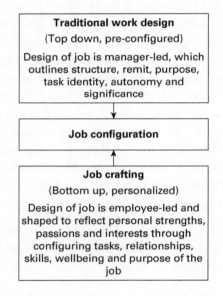

An overview of job crafting

For HR and people leaders, I find it useful to explore three different elements of job crafting. These are illustrated in the different layers of Figure 3.2. At the centre are the three core benefits of job crafting for individuals and organizations alike, the next layer depicts five different types of job crafting and the outer layer lists key questions which can be used to prompt job crafting.

FIGURE 3.2 The different elements of job crafting

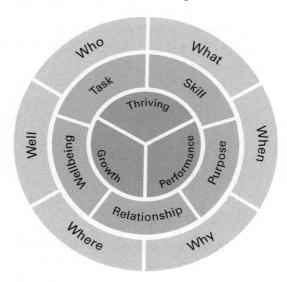

You could consider the three elements as the Why, the What and the How of job crafting. The Why relates to purpose and value, the What refers to job crafting's component parts and the How provides prompts to make job crafting happen.

Level 1 – why does job crafting matter?

The benefits of job crafting, from the perspectives of individuals, teams and organizations, can be grouped into three distinct categories – thriving, growth and performance. These will be explored in detail in Chapter 4, but a summary of each of these factors is given below.

THRIVING

Job crafting enables people to thrive in their work. It fosters positive individual measures of health, happiness, meaning and overall wellbeing and reduced levels of burnout, sickness absence, turnover and stress. Organizationally, job crafting has been found to positively influence job engagement, job satisfaction and retention.

GROWTH

Job crafting underpins and enables personal growth and development. Specifically, it nurtures people's abilities to develop their skills and knowledge and has been positively linked to a variety of measurements related to career progression and mobility.

PERFORMANCE

Job crafting has been positively linked to a variety of performance benefits. These include tangible measures of quality and quantity of output, ratings of performance given by line managers, self-assessment and peers, and higher levels of innovation and creativity.

Level 2 – what are the different types of job crafting?

Job crafting comes in different types, shapes and sizes. Building on research and practice, there are five core forms of job crafting that I make people leaders aware of, and encourage them to focus on, when looking to shape and personalize their approach to work. These elements include the original three types of job crafting (task crafting, relationship crafting and cognitive crafting) that Professors Amy Wrzesniewski and Jane Dutton wrote about in 2001.

TASK CRAFTING

Task crafting refers to tangibly shifting or changing the physical qualities of a job. For example, this would include adding, removing or redesigning activities, or reallocating time spent on different tasks and the order in which they might be carried out.

RELATIONSHIP CRAFTING

Relationship or relational crafting involves changing key social attributes, existing relationships and interactions. An example of relational crafting might include an employee increasing their social interactions with colleagues by volunteering to give tours of offices to new starters.

PURPOSE CRAFTING

Purpose crafting enables employees to reflect, alter and shift how they think about the significance and value of their work. As it is referring to changes to how people think about their work this has also been referred to as cognitive crafting. For example, a bank worker handling corporate accounts may cognitively re-craft their role by recognizing that they are providing a vital service to the wider local and national economy. Or a customer complaints handler could cognitively or purpose craft the meaning of their role as making the lives of customers better. By doing this they are aligning and changing how they see the purpose of their role.

SKILL CRAFTING

Skill crafting refers to making changes to skills and knowledge or the pursuit of learning opportunities at work for personal growth. This would include developing wider capabilities, exploring new skills, and specializing and developing knowledge in a specific area. Examples of skill crafting might include learning a new piece of software, technical knowledge or volunteering for a stretching project.

WELLBEING CRAFTING

Wellbeing crafting involves actively shaping the way a job is carried out to improve overall levels of individual health and wellbeing. Wellbeing-focused job crafting activity relates to finding ways to be more active, recharged, absorbed and engaged at work. An example of wellbeing crafting could be to have walking meetings, or getting outside every day.

Whilst the elements of job crafting are independent of each other, often job crafting activities will contain a number of different elements. For example, making a lunch date with a friend or colleague outside of the office would include elements of relationship (building connection) and wellbeing (getting outside and recharging) crafting. Similarly, undertaking a training course on presenting skills and consequently changing how you present at meetings would be an example of skill (consolidating or building a skill) and task crafting (changing the way you do aspects of your job). Chapter 5 will describe each of these different types in more detail.

Level 3 – how can you job craft?

Job crafting requires people to be curious about how their work is done and how it aligns to their individual strengths, passions and interests. Workers often spend 90–100 per cent of their time at work *doing* work without reflecting on *how* they are working. The following six questions encourage personal reflection on how work is being carried out and help to identify opportunities to subtly shift and change:

- **Who** do you interact and connect with during the course of your work?
- **What** are the different tasks and activities involved in your work?
- **Why** does your job exist? What is its purpose?
- **When** do you do different elements of your work? Are there opportunities to change these?
- How **well** do you feel at work? Are there opportunities to increase your wellbeing through the way you do and approach your job?
- **Where** do you perform your work? Would there be any possibility of, or benefit from, doing elements of your work in different locations?

These questions will be covered in greater detail in Chapter 6 where we will explore how to encourage job crafting in yourself and others.

Size and scale of job crafting

The make-up and nature of job crafting will vary depending on the needs and interests of the crafter together with contextual factors such as the demands and pressures of their work and the extent to which crafting and innovation are encouraged.

At the most extreme level, people can use job crafting to shape and develop entirely new jobs. One example that I often share with groups is of a team leader of the estates team at a large university. Following a Master's in Sustainability the team leader identified a series of opportunities to grow the sustainability agenda on the campus. Over time the work she was doing was given greater significance and recognition by the university. Subsequently, the university created a new Head of Sustainability role, which the individual competitively applied for and was appointed to. Another example is a marketing assistant working within a legal team. Following her interest in social media and communication she proactively started to develop the firm's online presence and over time this expanded into a full-time position which focused on external and social marketing.

In reality, job crafting seldom involves completely changing or transforming a job. The majority of job crafting is small, iterative and sometimes almost scrappy. People find and seize the opportunities when they present themselves to subtly change the job they are doing. To get a better understanding of the nature of job crafting that people undertook, I partnered with Dr Gavin Slemp from the University of Melbourne to analyse the examples I had collected from a series of job crafting workshops. Presenting our findings at the 2018 European Conference of Positive Psychology[6] on 63 different job crafting activities, we found that 77 per cent of job crafting examples were estimated to take less than 12 minutes a day or an hour a week, 21 per cent took over an hour a week but less than an hour a day, and only 2 per cent involved a change which took more than a day a week. Our analysis also showed that the majority of job crafting examples did not fundamentally alter the demands or load of the job. In total, 58 per cent of job crafting examples were neutral in terms of the impact on overall job workload, 38 per cent involved an increase in job demands and 4 per cent involved a decrease.

I often share these findings with leaders who are concerned about the implications of actively encouraging job crafting and the potential disruption that it may cause. A key insight from our study, which has been supported by subsequent research, is that people naturally tend to make small and subtle changes to their work through job crafting. These changes don't dramatically alter the demands, challenges or footprint of a job. This does not however mean that the impact of the changes on the job crafters themselves are also small. In my experience, the size of crafting is disproportionate to the benefits or impact. As we will explore, small changes can have a huge impact on engagement, happiness and performance.

Measuring job crafting

If you are curious about how much you currently job craft, one way to do this is through self-reflection. The box below includes a series of statements that I often use in job crafting workshops. These quickly allow people to gain some insight into their current crafting levels and the types of job crafting they might be doing.

HOW MUCH DO YOU JOB CRAFT?

To get a sense of how much you shape your work, read each sentence and think about how often you behave in the way described. Don't overthink your response. You can choose the time period you use to determine your answers, but you might find it helpful to think about how you worked in the last month.

Q1 I change my tasks so that they are more challenging. (Task crafting)

Q2 I add complexity to my tasks by changing their structure or sequence. (Task crafting)

Q3   I make efforts to get to know other people at work better. (Relationship crafting)

Q4   I try to spend more time with a wide variety of people at work. (Relationship crafting)

Q5   I think about ways in which my job as a whole contributes to society. (Purpose crafting)

Q6   I try to think of my job as a whole, rather than as separate tasks. (Purpose crafting)

Q7   I try to learn new things at work that go beyond my core skills. (Skill crafting)

Q8   I actively explore new skills to do my overall job. (Skill crafting)

Q9   I reflect on the role my job has in my overall health and wellbeing. (Wellbeing crafting)

Q10 I actively change the way I work to increase my health and wellbeing. (Wellbeing crafting)

These statements have been informed by validated job crafting scales and I would recommend that anyone interested in more fully and formally evaluating levels of job crafting consider these further.[7,8]

There are no wrong or right answers to these statements, and no such thing as good or bad levels of crafting. Everyone is different. The purpose of the questions, particularly when I use them in workshops, is to encourage people to start to consider the extent to which they currently shape and personalize their work. You might find that you undertake some elements of job crafting more than others. For example, you may actively try to change your tasks and activities (task crafting) but seldom actively connect to the purpose or meaning of your job (purpose crafting). The explanation for this may be a combination of your own motivations but also the opportunities which present themselves in your work.

My advice to people who ask about what type of job crafting they should undertake is to start small, experiment and craft in ways that they find most fun and interesting. Perhaps counterintuitively, I never stipulate that people focus on addressing areas where they don't currently job craft. In fact, if asked, I often advocate the opposite and recommend that people explore doing more of the activities that come naturally to them. I take this approach primarily for two reasons. First, at the heart of job crafting is proactive choice for people to shape their work in ways that they feel are worthwhile. Mandating or telling people what type of job crafting they should do takes away some of the control and autonomy. Second, by taking a strengths-based approach and leveraging existing talents and interests, people are more likely to be stimulated, engaged and ultimately successful in their job crafting goals. This in turn makes job crafting more likely to be an enjoyable and rewarding practice which will emerge into sustainable habits and positive changes in how they do their job.

Why do people craft their jobs?

Many people find that they do aspects of job crafting intuitively. They are naturally drawn to the desire to shape their work in ways which meet their individual needs and preferences. When thinking about the drivers for individual job crafting I find it's useful to consider five reasons which have been developed from my personal interviews with job crafters and existing research in this field.[9,10] There is some commonality and overlap between the drivers for job crafting and the broader motivations for personalization which we explored in Chapter 2.

Five key reasons that people job craft are:

1. Control

Employees deliberately shape their work to get a greater sense of control over all, or some, aspects of their jobs, in order to amplify positive and mitigate negative aspects. Using job crafting to boost a feeling of control is a reason why academics believe job crafting is positively linked with wellbeing, recognizing that a lack of control is a common source of stress and anxiety.

In my workshops people at all levels of seniority frequently comment about feeling a lack of control in their work – feeling that they are getting swept away or along with work, rather than being able to actively shape it.

EXAMPLE

Taking control of the day

A finance manager in a large consultancy firm used job crafting to bring back an element of control to her day. She explained to me in that whilst on the face of it she had significant levels of autonomy in terms of how she did her work, in reality her day was shaped by needs and requests from other people. It was filled with meetings and she faced a constant stream of communications, most of which needed her attention and sign-off. Consequently, she often only got around to the work she wanted to focus on at the end of the day when she was often mentally and physically tired. She saw job crafting as an opportunity to experiment with how she structured her day. The job crafting goal she set herself was to create space in the first 30 to 60 minutes of each day for time to plan, do deeper and more creative thinking and focus on any work that involved energy, attention and focus. She did this by blocking out any meeting requests before 10 am and tried not to check her email before this time either. She later explained to me in a follow-up meeting that she found starting the day in this way really beneficial. She found her productivity and sense of achievement increased and she felt a greater sense of control over her work.

2. Self-expression

People craft their jobs, to bring more of their whole and full selves to the work they are doing. It enables people to take off the masks that they might be wearing and hiding behind at work. A famous example of someone expressing himself through their work is David Holmes, a flight attendant for Southwest Airlines. David was described as Southwest Airlines' 'rhythmic ambassador',[11] because he had started to rap the pre-take off safety announcement once passengers were seated. When interviewed about this for CNN,[12] David said that he does it because it brings him joy and because he likes to have and bring fun to work. Whilst not everyone will want to rap at work as a way of self-expression, people often find job crafting provides an opportunity to project a positive sense of self in their own eyes and those of others.

EXAMPLE
Expressing gratitude

A project manager in a financial services organization set himself a job crafting goal of sending a note of thanks to members of his team at least once a week. He explained to me that the reason he had set this goal was because he was committed to being a positive and supportive team leader. By creating a more regular habit of expressing gratitude he was finding another mechanism through which to recognize the efforts of his colleagues and team members. A direct result of his job crafting goal was that a number of his colleagues had remarked that they had valued the personal notes of thanks he had sent them. Additionally, there were a number of unexpected outcomes too. The first was that he noticed that his colleagues had started to thank each other more, and second, he himself had found that he got a kick out of saying thank you to others – it made him feel happier in his job.

3. Connection

Nurturing and strengthening connections with other people is a third driver for job crafting. Humans are social creatures and we strive for opportunities for connection and positive interaction with others. High-quality and positive connections between people lead to greater physiological functioning (a strengthened cardiovascular, immune and neuroendocrine system), collaboration and engagement.[13] At the other extreme, poor, negative or abusive relationships can be detrimental to our wellbeing and ability to function. Job crafting enables and encourages people to shape and change the nature and content of interactions with others, to amplify the positive benefits of connection, whilst providing opportunities to reduce or reframe relationships that are not optimal.

Job crafting fulfils our need for a sense of connection and relatedness and mutual caring for other people. Consequently, people often set job crafting goals to build and foster relationships.

EXAMPLE
Building a bond with colleagues

A marketing manager for a consultancy firm had recently returned from maternity leave. In her absence the team she was working with had changed and she did not know many of the people in her new team. She identified that positive relationships with others were particularly important to her both in terms of her ability to do her job professionally as a marketing manager but also in terms of creating a sense of community and belonging for herself personally. Following a job crafting workshop she had set herself a 'secret' goal of finding out something new about one of her colleagues each day for a month. This fostered her sense of connection with people in her team and helped build up relationships with people she knew and those she didn't. She found it fun too.

---

4. Health and wellbeing

Job crafting empowers people to create conditions that allow them to positively influence their health and motivation at work.[14] It's common in job crafting workshops that a number of participants state a desire to create more opportunities to recharge and balance the demands of their work.

EXAMPLE

Bringing wellness into work

I recently delivered training to a group of physiotherapists and a number of them stated a desire to craft more opportunities for wellbeing into their work. Their days were demanding, often full of back-to-back clinics and calls with patients. They described that they often had little time to write up their notes, let alone time for opportunities to take a breath or recharge. Some examples of small job crafting experiments that they tested included: being diligent in taking a lunch break, taking a short walk outside around the building once a day, bringing healthy snacks into the office rather than cakes to keep their energy levels up, and practising mindful walking when moving from their offices to collect patients from reception.

5. Meaning

As we highlighted in Chapter 2, people are increasingly expressing a desire to have and find meaning in the work they are undertaking. Fundamentally, people want there to be a benefit from, and to see value in, the energy and effort they expend at work. For most people this sense of meaning relates to making a positive difference to others in some capacity.

EXAMPLE

A picture with meaning

A university theatre manager explained to me at a workshop in Australia why meaning in her work drove her desire to purpose craft. She explained that she looked at photos on her office wall which she had taken at past performances, when she was tired or doing some of the more laborious and administrative aspects of her work. The pictures she had taken were of the students high-fiving and jumping up and down after the curtain had gone down after a play. The theatre manager explained that creating opportunities for students to play and dance and feel joy and achievement were at the heart of why she did her job. She felt that the pictures captured all these elements, and were consequently a source of inspiration for her.

Is job crafting a fad?

In 2018 I was presenting at a regional CIPD conference. My session was in the afternoon and Rob Briner had given a barnstorming keynote in the morning. Rob is a Professor of Organizational Psychology at Queen Mary

University of London. He is a founding member of the Centre for Evidence-Based Management and regular keynote speaker on evidence-based practice and HR. His work has led him to be named as the 2018 most influential HR thinker by *HR Magazine*. Rob gave a fantastic talk on the need for evidence-based practice amongst organizations and HR in particular. Towards the end of his talk he focused on management fads. As he shared some ideas from management scholars on how to distinguish between an idea which was a management fad or a management classic,[15] my heart began to sink. A number of the factors he shared, on the face of it, applied to job crafting and were features of a presentation that I was going to give that afternoon.

The list that Rob presented on how to spot a likely fad included:

- It's buzzy and exciting – the concept claims to be completely new and novel but it is actually recycling an existing idea.
- There are massive claims made without good-quality supporting evidence.
- The concept is associated with management gurus and academic superstars.
- It's all good – there appear to be no downsides.
- It's a panacea – the concept works everywhere for everything for everyone.
- Evidence for the success of the concept comes from unverifiable anecdotes and success stories (usually big well-known companies whose success is attributed to the fad with no good evidence).
- The concept involves new buzz words which don't actually describe anything new.

Rather than ignore Rob's talk and present as planned, I decided to use the call to be more evidence-based and critical of new ideas and concepts as a positive. Hopefully, I thought, the audience would now be more curious about the content of my talk and the relevance and veracity of the information I was sharing.

I started the presentation by highlighting that some 'Fad' alarm bells might start to sound throughout the talk but that I was happy, confident and committed to explaining why I believed that job crafting was not a fad or fashion, but rather something that had inherent value. The talk was a success and a number of people came up to me afterwards to say that they had found it interesting to critically engage in a discussion about the evidence and research basis behind a concept or idea.

Here are the key reasons why I believe job crafting is not a fad:

1 **Job crafting is exciting, novel and new** – I certainly find job crafting an exciting and engaging topic. Whilst there have been references to employee-led work design prior to the conceptualization of job crafting, these have been fleeting[16] or related to other wider theories such as adjustments and transitions.[17] It was only after the publication of the first job crafting paper[18] that the concept was fully and carefully unpacked, conceptualized, studied and measured.

2 **There is a rich evidence base from research studies which underpins and substantiates job crafting** – Job crafting has been studied by researchers across the world involving a wide array of professions and sections. As of 2019 there have been over 130 empirical and peer-reviewed research papers[19] involving studies of tens of thousands of employees across the globe. This evidence base will be explored more in Chapter 4.

3 **Job crafting is not solely associated with high-profile and leading companies** – Whilst job crafting is a concept that has been used and encouraged at organizations such as Google, LinkedIn and Logitech it has also been successfully encouraged and observed in a wide array of different organizations, industries and sectors. Just because a high-profile company such as Google invests in job crafting, it certainly does not mean that other organizations should blindly look to follow suit. But organizations can use the experiences and reported results of other organizations to inform their own approach.

4 **Job crafting is not associated with one individual academic or management guru** – There are certainly consultants and researchers who have a specific interest and expertise related to job crafting. But one of the factors that I find makes job crafting compelling is that there are a broad array of professionals and academics who are exploring the concept and helping to build knowledge and experience about the benefits, and potential limitations, of the approach.

5 **It's not all good – there are clear limitations to job crafting** – Although there are clear benefits in taking a personalized approach to work, particularly given the right organizational and team context, there are limitations and potential negative aspects too. Fortunately, the majority of these limitations can be addressed or mitigated with appropriate foresight and planning.

6 **Job crafting is not a buzz word, but it does resonate** – There is no doubt that how a concept is named may influence how some people engage with or are drawn to it. In my experience, I find that job crafting resonates with people because it signals an approach which enables people to be more deliberate and personalized in their work. And the concept of

'crafting' is a term that is widely used to sell premium items from beers and coffees to holiday experiences. Rather than tapping into the current zeitgeist, job crafting as a term was first coined by Professors Amy Wrzesniewski and Jane Dutton when they started to draft their research in 1999. And in fact, job crafting was only a working and temporary title for the concept, but it ultimately stuck and the rest is history.

Conclusion

Whilst many organizations strive to be great places to work, many struggle to deliver on this promise and often don't create environments that enable people to bring their whole and full selves to work each day. Job crafting provides an easy, employee-led and evidence-based mechanism to do this, in a way that amplifies the existing strengths, talents and interests of the workforce. There are five distinct, but often complementary and overlapping, job crafting types: task, relationship, wellbeing, skill and purpose.

Whilst the broad notion and idea of people shaping their work to better align themselves with their personal needs and interests may not be entirely new in terms of work design theory, job crafting is a unique approach which describes employee-led proactivity. To date the research is compelling in terms of the benefits of job crafting.

For HR and people leaders curious about the strength of the evidence underpinning job crafting, and the benefits and drawbacks of this approach, the next chapter will provide a summary of the research into the short- and long-term outcomes, benefits and limitations of job crafting.

KEY POINTS

- Job crafting is a bottom-up, proactive, personalized and employee-led approach to work design.

- The key benefits of job crafting can be summarized as thriving, growth and performance.

- Five key types of job crafting are: task, relationship, purpose, skill and wellbeing.

- Job crafting involves people exploring how their work is done and how it aligns to their personal strengths, motivations and needs.

- The key reasons that people job craft are: control, connection, health, meaning and self-expression.

KEY QUESTIONS

- Have you ever job crafted?

- Have you ever witnessed other people job crafting?

- Are there any types of job crafting (task, relationship, wellbeing, purpose, skill) that you feel would be easier to do in your organization than others?

- What do you feel are the key strengths of job crafting and what are the limitations?

CASE STUDY

Logitech – design your impact

Founded in Switzerland in 1981 and quickly expanding to Silicon Valley, Logitech designs and produces personal peripherals to connect customers to their digital experiences. The chances are if you've used a computer or tablet, you've used a Logitech mouse, keyboard or driver at some point.

Logitech has a commitment to creating and sustaining a work environment that enables people to bring their full potential to their work. In 2016, Logitech was named as the grand prize winner of the prestigious Positive Business Project competition, run by the Center for Positive Organizations at the University of Michigan. Logitech's award was in recognition of their pioneering approach to developing people and a key part of this was creating opportunities for employees to explore job crafting through an organization-wide programme entitled Design Your Impact.

The purpose of the Design Your Impact session was to enable people to explore their personal strengths and values and to shape their work in ways that enabled them to bring their full selves to the workplace. As Jessica Amortegui, who was at the time Head of Global Learning and Development, explained to me: 'We wanted to give people an opportunity to be the architects and builders of their jobs, rather than being tied to one-size-fits-all job descriptions.' Logitech did this through a series of 90-minute workshops on job crafting where people were encouraged to explore ways to align their personal strengths and passions to what they were doing each day at work. Attendance at the sessions was voluntary but they proved popular, with over 2,000 of Logitech's 3,000 colleagues attending a Design Your Impact session, including senior executives. The workshops were held at over 10 different global sites, with opportunities and arrangements made for people to undertake the training in offsite locations too.

In terms of impact, Jessica confirmed in an interview in Michelle McQuaid's *Making Positive Psychology Work* podcast:[20]

What we found was that by helping someone to make micro-changes in the way they were working, the mix of tasks they were doing and who they were spending time with, we were able to have a mega impact on their levels of passion and engagement.

Logitech recognized that small changes were the key to unlocking changes in behaviour, and that the small marginal gains achieved spilled over into the job through both enjoyment and performance. To enable people to maximize opportunities for crafting, Jessica and the team were conscious of the ecosystem in which people were working and noted in a follow-up discussion with me that:

It's unrealistic to expect people to make changes simply based on a one-off intervention or workshop. You need to think about the wider organizational factors which will support the ideas and concepts you are trying to explore.

Logitech recognized that leaders were critical to empowering people to job craft. Consequently, in addition to the workshops, which many team leaders themselves attended, managers were separately sent information and resources about job crafting, its benefits and how they could encourage people's efforts to personalize their work. Leaders were also able to attend a short presentation about job crafting and its benefits. Jessica and the team found that this leadership support paid dividends and that job crafting was more successful when managers had meaningful conversations with their people about the ways they wanted to shape their work going forward.

Logitech were also pragmatic about the fact that job crafting does not suit everyone. Jessica told me:

You can't make people craft, and for a number of reasons, people may not have the energy or interest in shaping their work; instead you are better working with the people who are excited by the idea of exploring how to make their work better. It doesn't mean you should ignore people who can't craft or leave them behind; you need to support these people's development and growth in other ways.

Notes

1 Nesterak, E (2014) Google re:Work: shaping the future of HR, *Behavioural Scientist*, available at: https://behavioralscientist.org/google-rework-shaping-future-hr/ (archived at https://perma.cc/45ZE-KHWY)

2 Wrzesniewski, A (2015) Job crafting and creating meaning in your work, *re:Work*, available at: https://rework.withgoogle.com/blog/job-crafting-and-creating-meaning-in-your-work/ (archived at https://perma.cc/27LV-LCZ4)

3 Ibid

4 Berg, J M, Wrzesniewski, A and Dutton, J E (2010) Perceiving and responding to challenges in job crafting at different ranks: when proactivity requires adaptivity, *Journal of Organizational Behavior*, **31** (2–3), pp 158–86

5 Oldham, G and Hackman, J (2010) Not what it was and not what it will be: the future of job design research. *Journal of Organizational Behavior*, **31** (2–3), pp 463–79

6 AK Congress (2019) Book of abstracts: 9th European Conference on Positive Psychology, available at: https://static.akcongress.com/downloads/ecpp/ecpp2018_book_of_abstract.pdf (archived at https://perma.cc/2GAX-DZ9M)

7 Slemp, G S and Vella-Brodrick, D A (2013) The job crafting questionnaire: A new scale to measure the extent to which employees engage in job crafting, *International Journal of Wellbeing*, **3**, 126–46

8 Bindl, U K *et al* (2018) Job crafting revisited: implications of an extended framework for active changes at work, *Journal of Applied Psychology*, **104** (5), pp 605–28

9 Petrou, P *et al* (2012) Crafting a job on a daily basis: contextual correlates and the link to work engagement. *Journal of Organizational Behavior*, **33** (8), pp 1120–41

10 Wrzesniewski, A and Dutton, J E (2001) Crafting a job: revisioning employees as active crafters of their work, *Academy of Management Review*, **26** (2), 179–201

11 Southwest Airlines (2009) The GAAP RAP by Southwest Airlines rapping flight attendant, *YouTube*, available at: https://www.youtube.com/watch?v=7P2-vEtXSug (archived at https://perma.cc/N4P4-BV7X)

12 CNN (2011) The Southwest Airlines safety rap by flight attendant David Holmes, *YouTube*, available at: https://www.youtube.com/watch?v=fNU0M2dG5h8 (archived at https://perma.cc/PEU8-3MTP)

13 Heaphy, E D and Dutton, J E (2008) Positive social interactions and the human body at work: Linking organizations and physiology, *Academy of Management Review*, **33** (1), pp 137–62

14 Petrou, P *et al* (2012) (see note 9 above)

15 Miller, D, Hartwick, J and Le Breton-Miller, I (2004) How to detect a management fad – and distinguish it from a classic, *Business Horizons*, **47** (4), pp 7–16

16 Heaphy, E D and Dutton, J E (2008) (see note 13 above)

17 Petrou, P *et al* (2012) (see note 9 above)

18 Wrzesniewski, A and Dutton, J E (2001) (see note 10 above)

19 Lichtenthaler, P W and Fischbach, A (2019) A meta-analysis on promotion- and prevention-focused job crafting, *European Journal of Work and Organizational Psychology*, **28** (1), pp 30–50

20 McQuaid, M (nd) Can you teach someone to love their job? Available at https://www.michellemcquaid.com/can-teach-someone-love-job/ (archived at https://perma.cc/3CL7-AEM3)

04

The benefits of and evidence for job crafting

The why of job crafting

'So what?' is, I find, a useful and important question to ask whenever anyone is presenting a new initiative, concept or idea. It is certainly something I get challenged on when I am speaking to people about job crafting. And I welcome the question. In fact, I'm always slightly concerned if people appear to take everything I say on face value, without testing the evidence base that sits behind the ideas I share, or testing any limitations or potential side effects. In response to the 'so what' question, I start by sharing that job crafting supports individuals, teams and organizations to thrive, grow and perform (see Figure 4.1).

From my perspective these three terms best describe 'the why' of job crafting and are useful umbrella themes from which to explore, in more detail, different known benefits of shaping and customizing work.

The focus of this chapter will be to explore and unpack each of these three elements, outlining the breadth and depth of research in each area and how it applies to organizations and specifically HR and people leaders.

Thriving

The first key benefit strand of job crafting is thriving. Job crafting enables people to alter the content of their job in ways that can cultivate a positive sense of meaning and identity in the work they do. By doing this, workers move from a generic 'ready-made' job role to an individualized way of working that creates a sense and source of positive meaning and self-expression

FIGURE 4.1 The benefits of job crafting

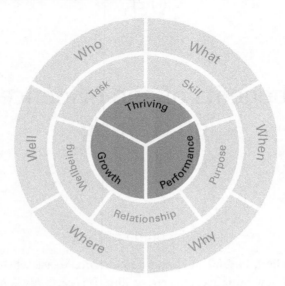

which strengthens psychological wellbeing and overall thriving. Thriving employees have control over, and a sense of purpose, engagement and enjoyment in, the work they do. They feel good and function well and their levels of wellbeing are high.

Happiness and positive emotions

Job crafting enables people to shape their work experiences to spend more time or focus on activities and aspects of their work they enjoy and find fulfilling. A 2012 study by Professor Amy Wrzesniewski and colleagues with a Fortune 500 technology company found that job crafting was positively related to short-term boosts in happiness.[1] Participating in a job crafting workshop led employees to be significantly happier and more effective in their jobs six weeks later, based on ratings from their peers and managers.

Spending more time doing the things that we value feels good and bolsters our happiness and enjoyment in our work. And the blend of activities which furnish us with positive emotions will be different for each of us. I'm always fascinated by the different types of work that bring people a sense of happiness and joy. Some of the enjoyable tasks that people have shared with me in workshops and discussions include giving presentations, coding, developing Excel spreadsheets and databases, photocopying, dealing with customer complaints, developing new ideas, washing pipettes, cleaning, writing strategic documents and greeting visitors. My takeaway from this is that different people enjoy different things. I know this is not a profound realization, but it is certainly something that, disappointingly, many organizations fail to explore or understand.

Engagement

Whilst we might physically keep our eyes open for (most) of our waking day, how much of our time would we describe as being totally focused, engaged and excited? For the majority of us, we find our attention increasingly splintered and split and our motivations in flux.

Job crafting nurtures engagement and focus in tangible and intangible ways. Research has consistently linked job crafting to higher levels of overall job engagement[2,3] and satisfaction.[4,5,6] The key explanation for this is that proactively personalizing aspects of their jobs enables people to nudge their work in ways and directions that provide more enjoyment and encourage more energy focus and absorption in their tasks. Relatedly, job crafting has been linked to vigour, dedication and absorption[7,8,9] in work activities. Vigour refers to feeling energetic and a willingness to put higher levels of discretionary effort into a task and is associated with a desire to continue working even in the face of challenge and adversity. Dedication refers to an individual's enthusiasm underpinned by a sense of the work being meaningful and inspiring. Absorption refers to the extent to which an individual becomes fully emerged and focused on a task or activity.

Wellbeing

There is growing recognition of the importance of individual wellbeing and health inside and outside of workplaces. People feel good about and perform well in their work when they have high levels of physical and mental health. Job crafting has been found to be related to positive wellbeing[10] as well as reduced levels of burnout[11,12], job strain[13] and depression.[14] By shaping the design of their jobs, workers are able to meet their needs for control over their jobs, develop positive emotions and self-image, establish connections with others, and furnish a deeper connection to the meaning of the work they do. These fulfil fundamental human needs in a positive way, which in turn underpins and fosters wellbeing.

Meaning

Work, as the author and historian Louis 'Studs' Terkel wrote in the introduction of his seminal 1974 book *Working,*[15] is 'a search for daily meaning as well as daily bread'. This was a conclusion he had reached following interviews with over 100 different male and female workers in a variety of jobs from across the United States. The challenge of finding meaning in work was perhaps best summed up by one of Terkel's interviewees, Nora Watson, an editor and staff writer, who said, 'Most of us… have jobs that are too small for our spirit. Jobs are not big enough for people.'

At the heart of meaningful work is the belief that the work we are doing matters. It involves a sense of belonging to, or service of, something that we believe in which is greater than ourselves. Unfortunately, many jobs don't come with meaning pre-packed into them, and people need to find this for themselves. One way to find and develop this sense of meaning is to proactively shape it into our work and a number of studies have demonstrated that job crafting can help people to find and create meaning in their work in this way.[16] Proactively tailoring work enables people to move from a generic 'ready-made' job role to an individualized and personalized way of working that creates a sense and source of positive meaning and self-expression.

A simple but powerful way that job crafting boosts and embeds meaning is to encourage people to explore the impact of the work they do and how it helps other people.[17] For example, a project or change manager could do this by intentionally spending time connecting with and getting to know the teams and individuals who their work will influence. Crafting in this way would enable the manager to establish a deeper understanding of the positive (and sometimes negative) consequences of their work on other people.

Whole teams can benefit from hearing directly from the people they support. For example, to foster more opportunities to understand how they were helping others, an HR team working for a professional service company brought together different stakeholders from the business to hear stories about the value that HR had provided to them individually or to their team. Sharing and hearing these examples directly from the beneficiaries of their work gave people from across the HR team an opportunity to reflect and tap into the significance and purpose of their individual and collective jobs.

Relationships

The frequency and quality of our connections with those around us, including family, friends, colleagues and neighbours, have a profound impact on our health, wellbeing and ability to thrive. It is in the company of others that we often experience pleasure, share jokes and joy, are given companionship, support, love and kindness. Strong social networks not only foster thriving, but also can act as a buffer against stress and anxiety.

The greater the quality, frequency and length of the connections we make, the better we tend to function. This is applicable to all aspects of our lives, including work. Relationship crafting enables people to build and amplify existing and new relationships.

EXAMPLE
Building connections in a call centre

One of my favourite examples of how relationship job crafting has been used to build connections comes from a customer service call centre team of a large bank. As a result of job crafting training, and in the spirit of disrupting and trying new things, one of the colleagues suggested that rather than having a standard team meeting, they make the most of the good weather outside (a rarity in their location in a north-east corner of England) to play a game of rounders. It was a memorable and significant event for the team and was the first time that they had had both the permission and enthusiasm to try something spontaneous and different. Taking a risk and doing something different not only fostered relationships, but showed the benefits of trying something novel and new. When I went to visit the team a few weeks after the game to discuss their experiences of job crafting, people were excited to share their experiment with me. They were still smiling and joking about it when they did so and I noticed that people had even printed pictures out of the game and they were plastered around the office. The time it took to play the game was about 90 minutes, but it appeared to have had a profound effect. It was a credit to the team leader that they allowed and enabled the team to do something so different to the more traditional team meetings and get-togethers. I'm also convinced that if the team leader had suggested the game, it would not have been so warmly embraced. The fact that members of the team had come up with the idea themselves and it was such a significant departure from 'normal' ways of working appeared to make it all the more powerful.

Accomplishment

Accomplishment

Accomplishment develops from working towards or reaching a goal and having the self-motivation, grit and tenacity to see it through. A sense of accomplishment fosters wellbeing and thriving through the positive feelings associated with doing something, and doing it well. Job crafting gives people the opportunities to generate this sense of achievement by meeting their job crafting goals.

EXAMPLE
Crafting accomplishment

A Chief People Officer commented to me that setting and completing their job crafting goal had given them an opportunity to be more deliberate and conscious about how they performed aspects of their work. This individual had created a goal of finding time to speak to and check in with her colleagues every day. Every time and each day they did this it generated a sense of achievement. Similarly, a physiotherapist who decided to use the 10-minute walk into work to listen to a specialist podcast commented to me that not only were they learning something, but they felt good about achieving the positive job crafting goal they had set themselves.

Growth

The second key benefit of job crafting is personal and professional growth. Job crafting enables people to develop themselves, their colleagues and their work. By shaping and changing how work is undertaken, people are effectively undertaking a series of small and progressive change experiments. Trying new things, exploring what works and what doesn't and reflecting on how work aligns to current and future interests, motivations and ambitions all fuel personal, professional and organizational progression.

Skills and knowledge

Job crafting enables people to consolidate, build and amplify their strengths, skills and knowledge.[18] By choosing job crafting activities which build personal resources, people are able to support their personal growth and development. When researchers investigated the nature and type of job crafting that people naturally take, resource-building and growth activities were found to represent 34 per cent of the activities.[19]

Growth activities could include seeking feedback, learning new skills, on-the-job and formal training and learning. Someone volunteering for a new project or challenging piece of work which will stretch them or consolidate existing skills are examples of job crafting that will foster development.

EXAMPLE
Building skills and knowledge

A specific example from HR that I have encountered of building skills and knowledge was a manager volunteering to lead the investigation for a high-profile and complex employee relations case in order to stretch themself both technically, in terms of case law and procedures, and more broadly in terms of managing organizational risk. An example of someone doing an existing task in a new way includes a marketing manager who described how they experimented with not using slide decks in presentations to their team because they wanted to stop their reliance on technology and foster connection with others. A computer programmer learning a new programming language is a type of skill crafting where someone is actively learning a new skill.

Career mobility

Job crafting has been found to benefit individual career progression, often because people who job craft create, or are open to, new ways to develop and demonstrate key skills, strengths and talents. The most common and convincing explanation offered for job crafting's positive influence on career progression is that it helps to create a better fit between the individual and their job, enabling them to express their values and beliefs whilst also using their strengths and expertise. Empirical studies – those based on observations and experiments – have found that job crafting supports a variety of outcomes linked to career progression. These include overall employability,[20] career competence[21] (the skills, knowledge and abilities needed for career development), career satisfaction (positive feelings about the progress of one's career) and career motivation[22] (motivation to progress career).

Job crafting is positively related to promotions too. A study by Roberto Cenciotti, Guido Alessandri and Laura Borgogni from Sapienza University of Rome, monitored 349 middle managers from one of the largest service organizations in Italy. Participants were tracked over a two-year period. People who job crafted more were found to be more likely to have positive feelings of career success and also more likely to have received promotions within the company.[23]

Performance

The third key broad benefit of job crafting relates to performance. Job crafting enables people to align their work in ways that best fits their strengths, talents and interests, and in doing so enables them to undertake their work in ways that create the best opportunities for them to deliver optimum performance.

Job and task performance

There have been a number of specific job crafting studies investigating how job crafting supports performance in various professional contexts. For example, job crafting has been linked to higher quality of care in childcare centres,[24] hospitals[25] and nursing homes,[26] greater teaching performance[27] and more call time spent and increased donations raised in a fundraising organization.[28] Job crafting has been linked to better overall performance in diverse settings including car manufacturing,[29] chemical plants[30] and Fortune 500 technology companies.[31]

More broadly, a 2018 review of 28 empirical job crafting studies found a positive relationship between performance and job crafting.[32] Whilst there were inconsistencies of the measurements of job crafting and performance used within the studies they evaluated, the authors were able to conclude that (p 305):

> Job crafting research also holds practical implications for HRD [HR] practitioners who are tasked with improving employees' and organizations' performance... HRD practitioners can increase employees' performance and wellbeing by facilitating job crafting behaviours and helping them [employees] to develop the knowledge and skills that are necessary for their expanded tasks.

The authors believed that the reason for this increase in performance was because crafting allowed people to improve the fit between their jobs and their individual needs and preferences, which eliminated inefficiencies and work frustrations whilst expanding skills and fuelling motivation and satisfaction.

A 2019 meta-analysis of job crafting interventions published in the *European Journal of Work and Organizational Psychology*[33] investigated the estimated return on investment in terms of increased performance as a result of job crafting workshops and interventions. The researchers concluded that the average dollar increase in output was $2,310 per employee after three months (with variance between $1,010 and $3,610), which corresponded to an average increase in performance per employee after three months of 14 per cent.

Innovation

It's challenging for a company to stay innovative if everyone's way of working remains unaltered. We are creatures of habit, and most companies tend to be bureaucracies that impose and praise order and consistency. This leads to a default of people getting stuck in their day-to-day tasks without having the energy or encouragement to take a step back and see opportunities to innovate and improve how they do their jobs and the way their work is designed.

Job crafting is a way to enable people to shake up their established ways of working and to identify and experiment with new combinations in terms of how they do their job. It is perhaps therefore not surprising that job crafting as a form of creative problem solving has been positively linked with innovation and creativity.[34,35,36] For example, a study of over 600 workers from a variety of occupations and industries in the United States by Uta Bindl *et al* found that as people crafted their work they also created opportunities to be more innovative.[37] Examples of how people were observed innovating their approach to work as a consequence of job crafting included: incorporating new and novel ways of working and tackling tasks; building collaborations and relationships with colleagues which led to the production of new ideas; and focusing on skills and applying strengths that enable people to be more creative. These results were supported in a separate but complementary study that the same researchers, led by Uta Bindl, undertook with 388 participants from a variety of occupations recruited in the UK.[38] Again, job crafting was positively linked to innovation at work and the ability to develop and implement new ideas and ways of working. Other studies have observed that job crafting has unlocked ideas amongst employees that have opened up opportunities for the company to develop new products, ideas and markets.[39]

Customer satisfaction

The benefits and impact of job crafting often extend beyond the individual job crafter. A study by Mushtaq A Siddiqi[40] explored the connection between job crafting and customer experience. Combining his experience of working in the banking sector and his PhD in service marketing, Mushtaq set out to investigate the link between job crafting and customer satisfaction and loyalty. The study involved public, private and foreign banks operating in the north of India, including Delhi, Punjab and Haryana.

As part of the experiment, bank employees were asked to complete a survey which measured, amongst other factors, job crafting. For each worker, a number of customer service scores were collected. A total of 203 employees completed the study and an average of 2.7 satisfaction reports were collected from customers for each employee. The study found a positive relationship between job crafting and the satisfaction and loyalty scores given to them by their customers. This was particularly the case for workers who crafted their work in ways that fostered social connection and support.

An explanation for the positive relationships between personalizing work and greater satisfaction from customers is that people who craft their work may be more motivated and satisfied in their jobs and this energy and enthusiasm spills over to the support and service they deliver to their customers. Similarly, when people are able to focus on aligning work in ways that use their strengths and talents, they will be better placed and able to deliver high-quality work which will be for the betterment and benefit of customers.

Organizational change

Job crafting encourages and enables employees to be curious about how they can make changes to their jobs and the work they do. People who feel encouraged and enabled to job craft are well placed to seize the opportunities and manage the challenges which present themselves during times of transformation and change.

Research has shown that whilst job crafting enables people to positively respond to organizational change, the type of crafting that people do is influenced by their motivations at work and the quality of communications and updates they receive about change. A 2016 study of 368 police officers investigated the nature of job crafting people undertook in response to organizational change.[41] The types of changes being faced by participants included the merging of departments, staff relocations and the transition to new information and communication systems. The police officers were asked to complete a survey which measured a number of factors including job crafting, their perceptions of the quality of change communication by the organization, work engagement and adaptability.

The study found that clearly communicated change plans fostered positive job crafting and this was particularly the case for people who were typically creative and extraverted and motivated by opportunities to grow themselves and their roles. These individuals saw organizational change as an opportunity for growth and proactively shaped their roles and ways of working to embrace new opportunities. By contrast, when communication plans were poor or unclear, employees with a focus on safety and security (referred to as prevention-focused employees by the researchers) used job crafting to seek clarity and a sense of control over their work.

One takeaway from the study is that people may use job crafting in different ways, such as coping with the changes or maximizing opportunities for growth and progression, depending on their personal perceptions about the benefits or threats of transformation and the quality of information about the change provided by the organization. For companies with clear plans and agendas, job crafting could be a useful mechanism to enable people to cope with and positively respond to change. And this is particularly the case where people feel clearly informed and are regularly updated about the changes being planned and carried out.

Research into job crafting strengths and limitations

Strength and depth of research

Job crafting is an example of an academically developed concept which can be easily applied and translated to workplaces. A strength of job crafting research is the depth and breadth of studies that have been published. A 2019 meta-analysis of empirical job crafting research included over 130 empirical and peer-reviewed research papers[42] involving studies from around the world. The impact of job crafting has been investigated with employees from Australia, Brazil, China, Finland, Germany, Greece, Italy, Netherlands, Portugal, Turkey, the United Kingdom, the United States and Vietnam.[43] In total, studies of job crafting have included the combined investigation of over 46,750 employees.[44] Job crafting has been empirically explored in a variety of different contexts, settings and industries ranging from cleaners and call centre operatives to change architects and chief executives, from public to private sectors and from automotive manufacturers to zoos.

FIGURE 4.2 Citations of the original 2001 job crafting paper

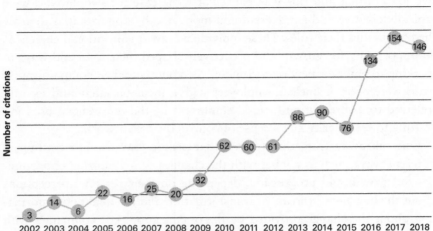

The study of job crafting has also been steadily growing and has been undertaken by researchers from a variety of distinct, but complementary academic discipline areas. These include the fields of Leadership, Management, Human Resources, Occupational Psychology, Work Psychology and Positive Psychology. To get a sense of the growth of interest and research into job crafting, Figure 4.2 plots the number of citations per year since the 2001 publication of the first paper on job crafting. This paper would typically be included in any study or research paper on job crafting using the Web of Science™.[45] This study by Amy Wrzesniewski and Jane Dutton had been cited over 1,075 times by 2018.

Research limitations

Whilst I believe the research into job crafting is compelling, it is important to be both careful and critical in appraising its strength. We can say with confidence from current research studies that job crafting is consistently and credibly related to a number of positive outcomes and benefits using refined statistical analysis. But it is important to recognize that the research does not allow us to say that job crafting itself causes or directly leads to these outcomes. The nature of studies outside laboratories and within organizations limits the scope and opportunity for experiments to be designed and carried out that would irrefutably prove the causal impact of job crafting. Unfortunately, it's not possible to use double-blind studies and inject people with a dose of job crafting and stand back and measure what happens in the way that might be possible with medical studies.

A further limitation of business, management and human resource studies is that they tend to be both one-off and one of a kind. The types of organizations and job roles in which the studies take place often differ and the experimental protocols and measurements, whilst similar, are rarely exactly the same. Whilst this gives people curious about the benefits of job crafting a diverse pool of studies to draw from it can make comparisons difficult and studies almost impossible to replicate in terms of the make-up of participants.

So whilst I have confidence in the research I have shared it is important, as with any new idea or concept, to be curious and critical about the evidence presented and how it might apply to yourself or your organizational context. In Chapter 8 we will explore further the evidence-based decision making in relation to HR and job crafting in more depth.

TWO JOB CRAFTING RESEARCH PERSPECTIVES

1. Crafting a better fit

To date, the research on job crafting has been built upon two contrasting but complementary perspectives. The conceptualization of job crafting by Professors Amy Wrzesniewski and Jane Dutton from their 2001 study has encouraged a focus based on an employee's motivation to create a better and more meaningful work experience for themselves. From this perspective, three core types of job crafting were identified:

- task crafting (such as changing tasks and activities);
- relationship crafting (such as spending time building or changing relationships with others);
- cognitive crafting (such as spending time reflecting on the purpose and value of a job).

By making changes to these three aspects, employees alter how work is experienced and can shift work toward personal preferences, needs and motives. Over time, other types of job crafting, such as skill and wellbeing crafting, have been added to this original list.

2. Crafting better balance between job demands and resources

The second dominant job crafting perspective focuses on proactive shaping and tailoring the demands and resources of a job and the abilities of employees to balance these with their personal needs, passions and abilities.[46] Job demands are aspects of work that require the expenditure of energy, focus and attention such as physical, emotional and mental effort. Job resources are aspects of work that replenish, stimulate and grow – they enable personal growth and development and underpin and fuel performance. The researchers Maria Tims and Arnold Bakker[47] proposed that employees could job craft in four different ways:

- increasing structural resources (such as seeking out opportunities to develop knowledge);
- increasing social resources (such as seeking support and feedback from a colleague or supervisor);
- increasing challenging job demands (such as taking on additional duties and responsibilities);
- decreasing hindering job demands (such as diminishing aspects of work or interactions that are particularly stressful or negative).

At the core of both job crafting perspectives is a shared focus on employees being proactive in shaping or changing their work to meet their needs. A key point of difference between the two research camps relates to the reasons which drive this change: a desire for greater fit with motivations, meaning and identity from the Wrzesniewski and Dutton perspective, or finding an equilibrium between the challenges and opportunities of a job and personal needs.

My approach to encouraging and enabling job crafting draws from and builds upon elements of both perspectives. I encourage people when exploring job crafting to consider their strengths, passions and aspirations as well as ensuring the right level of tension between the demands their work places on them and the opportunities for growth and development.

The potential dark side of job crafting

When I speak about job crafting, I often get asked about drawbacks and the negative consequences. And whilst the majority of job crafting research has reported favourable outcomes, it is important to acknowledge that in certain circumstances job crafting has the potential to be detrimental for the individual crafter or the organization in which they are working. The negative impacts or side-effects of job crafting relate to:

- crafting in unfavourable ways that don't suit the organization;
- crafting in ways that negatively impact others;
- negative experiences of job crafting; and
- lack of support and mixed messages.

Fortunately, with care and attention, these negative aspects of job crafting can be avoided, particularly if people are encouraged to craft in wise ways by their leaders.

Crafting in unfavourable ways

When I deliver job crafting workshops to leaders I often get a mixed reception. Whilst there are some people who are excited about the idea and want to share it with their colleagues, others are often more sceptical, and I can feel them weighing up the benefits and costs of supporting the approach. My advice to leaders is that they are almost always better off asking people to job craft openly with encouragement rather than covertly without management support. By being open to the idea, leaders are better able to enable crafting in ways that are mutually beneficial to the employee, their team and the wider organization.

In my discussions with Professor Amy Wrzesniewski, she confirms that she has had similar experiences and if anything she has stronger advice. In presentations with business leaders she often calls out the job crafting elephant in the room. She will tell groups:

> For those who think this is a terrible idea and this doesn't go in my organization and I don't want my employee doing this, I have good and bad news. The good news is that I have a lot to offer you because people will job craft whether you give them permission or not. The bad news is that for those [leaders] who try to ignore job crafting, your employees will hide it from you – they'll go underground.

Leaders who are asking if they can stop job crafting or shaping their work are asking the wrong question. Fundamentally, it's not in their control to do this. The question leaders need to ask themselves, according to Professor Wrzesniewski, is: 'Do you want people to be job crafting in secret, or do you want people to work in ways where they can adopt and maximize ways of working that really work for them and enable them to thrive?'

Negatively impacting others

A further concern raised by managers is that someone might job craft in ways that benefits them as an individual but either directly or indirectly negatively impacts on their colleagues. For example, if someone finds keeping project logs up to date a real drag and decides to stop doing it then this may impede other people's ability to understand whether certain aspects of a project have been delivered or not. Similarly, someone could decide to stop or indiscriminately delegate aspects of their work and expect others to pick them up. To avoid job crafting negatively impacting on other people I recommend that when people job craft they think about the impact of their proposed changes on others and ideally involve their colleagues in a discussion and seek their agreement. For example, if someone in customer services simply job crafts by ignoring phone calls because they don't like confrontation then this may lead to others in the team having to pick up more calls, or even customer calls going unanswered. This would clearly be a negative outcome for the organization (and of course the customer on the unanswered end of the telephone). One advantage of job crafting workshops with teams is that they create opportunities to openly discuss and share their job crafting ideas with others before they try them out.

EXAMPLE
Seeking permission from colleagues to swap tasks

One example of the benefits of teams discussing their job crafting ideas before implementing them comes from a workshop I ran with a central function at a bank. Through discussions about different aspects of their work, the group started talking about team meetings. One of the participants (Eva) confessed that she hated when it was 'her turn' to take minutes at the meetings. Exploring this further it turned out that, for reasons no one could remember, the team took it in turns to write notes about the meeting and to chase up agreed actions. For her job crafting goal Eva asked colleagues whether in return for not taking notes (a detail-oriented task that drained her energy), she could instead organize a monthly team social outing or activity, something that leveraged her strengths for building relationships. People were happy with this proposed swap – it turned out that there were a number of Eva's colleagues who got twitchy if notes from meetings were not being taken and were happy to follow up actions. These colleagues gladly volunteered to do more agenda coordinating and action noting. This example, whilst small, is important. Many of us, like Eva, will have unspoken frustrations or energy drainers that we don't have the opportunity or courage to share with others. In Chapter 7 we will explore ways to enable and support these types of discussions through exercises and 'job swaps'.

Negative and unexpected outcomes

Part of the reason I think people should approach and think about job crafting as a form of experimentation is that no one, including the crafter themself, knows what the outcomes will be in respect of the changes they make. You have to make the change, and then see what differences it makes and whether it is something that is beneficial.

Sometimes the outcomes of job crafting are unexpected. For example, taking on additional tasks or volunteering for a new project might lead to some benefits in terms of learning, but these could be outweighed by additional pressures and demands from taking on additional responsibilities. Similarly, when people reduce their demands by, for example, stopping doing or delegating activities, there would be an expectation that this would likely have a positive impact on the individual. This is not always the case, and in fact a number of studies have found that reducing job demands has actually reduced people's engagement and satisfaction with their work.[48,49] A potential explanation for this is that people may feel that by reducing and restricting elements of their work they are failing at their job (although of course this is often not the case) and start to view their work with negative emotions and feelings.

Mixed messages and job crafting getting blocked

The greatest risk with inviting and encouraging job crafting is not related to how people craft or the impact on others, but the soul-crushing consequence of blocking someone's attempt to craft. Hindering people's job crafting attempts either deliberately or inadvertently not only negates the positive benefits people get from crafting, but can negatively impact on people's level of motivation and engagement. In effect, you are creating false expectations and hope by, on the one hand, encouraging people to shape and personalize how they do their work, yet on the other, stifling opportunities to do this. From a motivational or engagement perspective this can be crippling to the employee and consequently disastrous to the organization in the longer term. As we explored in Chapter 2, there are serious and sustained consequences for people who develop feelings of helplessness and a lack of control in their jobs.

Fortunately, in my experience, the mismatch between espoused encouragement to craft at an organizational level and diminished or restricted opportunities to do this is not a frequent occurrence. When I have encountered this, it is most often because individual leaders or managers have not had the opportunity to fully understand job crafting or explore the concept for themselves. As a consequence, and perhaps understandably, some managers are naturally suspicious of attempts by people to proactively change their jobs and are nervous about the consequences of doing so. It is for this reason that information and training for leaders and managers is so critical in enabling job crafting on a sustained basis.

How to job craft 'wisely' – three key principles

I'm often asked by leaders for advice on how to ensure that employees job craft in ways that benefit the individual, their colleagues and the organization. The honest answer I give to leaders is that you can't control how people craft. But this doesn't mean you can't do anything. I recommend that leaders share with people guiding principles that employees can use to shape their crafting goals in 'wise ways'. I've developed these principles from the research of Professor Sharon Parker, Director of the Centre for Transformative Work Design at Curtin University. Professor Parker investigated 'wise proactivity', which was the term she used to describe proactive ways of working that promoted rather than hindered individual and organizational success.[50]

There are three factors that Professor Parker identified in her original study and I have adapted these for job crafting below:

a **Alignment – How does it align to the focus of your job and your organization?** When job crafting, leaders could encourage people to consider the extent to which their job crafting behaviour supports the overall strategy of the organization. If the job crafting goal doesn't support the strategy or isn't providing value to the individual then it is important to consider the utility of that job crafting activity.

b **Impact on others – How does it influence and impact on other people?** When job crafting, it is important to think about any implications for other stakeholders, such as team members, colleagues working in other areas of the organization and customers.

c **Impact on self – How will it influence your overall workload?** One of the easiest ways to job craft is to volunteer for new projects or to take on additional work tasks. People tend to be reluctant to reduce their work or stop doing certain tasks. The potential negative consequence of this is that people could be increasing the demands of their work through job crafting and creating additional work pressures which, if untested, could in the longer term lead to negative consequences. Job crafting goals should ideally enable people to work smarter, not harder, and employees should be careful to optimize their time to reach their goals in order to avoid an overload of stress and burnout.

WHAT CAN HR DO TO PROMOTE WISE PROACTIVITY AND JOB CRAFTING?

In an interview with the Australian HR Institute[51] (AHRI) Professor Sharon Parker highlighted three things that HR could do to nudge people towards 'wise' proactivity.

First, HR could encourage the flow and devolvement of information regarding organizational strategy, goals, timeframes and budgets. By doing this people are more likely to understand and identify any potential conflicts between job crafting behaviour and the wider objectives of the organization.

Second, Professor Parker suggests that HR can actively foster approaches to teamworking, which builds trust and collaboration. When people work in teams they are more likely to consider the impact of any changes to their jobs on their colleagues and minimize or avoid any negative consequences of job crafting or other proactive behaviour.

Third, Professor Parker outlines that HR needs be diligent in encouraging people to be proactive in healthy ways which buffer and minimize overload. She says, 'HR should, of course, care about burnout. Unfortunately, we're seeing something of an epidemic of mental health issues in the workplace.'

Conclusion

To date, whilst job crafting as a concept has grown in terms of academic research in the fields of HR, management and work psychology, it has not permeated into HR and people practice. There are a number of compelling benefits of job crafting which are relevant to HR and people leaders looking to create a workplace culture where people can sustainably and genuinely thrive, grow and perform. Despite these benefits, job crafting is not a panacea. There are a number of potential limitations and dark sides to personalizing work which can, whilst (relatively) easily mitigated, lead to problems for an individual and the wider organization. Creating an organizational and leadership approach and encouraging 'wise' job crafting are two ideas that can be particularly effective.

At this stage of the book, I hope you are, as I was when I first discovered job crafting, curious about exploring whether it is something that might be valuable for you individually, the teams and people you work with, and the organizations you work for. The focus of the next chapter will be how to encourage and bring job crafting to life.

KEY POINTS

- The key benefits ('the why') of job crafting can be summarized as Thriving, Growth and Performance.
- There are a number of potential negative consequences of job crafting to be aware of which include crafting in unfavourable ways, negatively impacting on others, and organizational inconsistency.
- 'Wise' job crafting principles encourage people to consider the impact of their job crafting on themselves, their colleagues and the direction and priorities of the organization.
- Globally, job crafting research has been undertaken across a wide range of service industries and sectors.
- Whilst, overall, job crafting research is compelling, it is important to be cautious and curious about the limitations of the research.

KEY QUESTIONS

- What do you see as the key benefits of job crafting?
- Are there any benefits of job crafting that are particularly relevant to your organization?
- What would be the key challenges or barriers to enabling job crafting in your organization?
- What questions do you have about the research to date and what do you want to explore further?

CASE STUDY
Crafting technology and transformation at Virgin Money

James McGlynn is the Chief Information Officer (CIO) of CYBG with responsibility for information, technology, transformation and data security at Virgin Money and CYBG. Whilst technology used to be a limiter in terms of functionality and agility for financial service organizations, it is now shaping and leading disruption and transformation of business processes, operations and service delivery.

In 2017, working with Jules Smith, Head of People Services, James commissioned a job crafting pilot with members of the CIO function. Attendees ranged from change leaders to fraud and financial crime managers. Participants attended a workshop run by Tailored Thinking, which introduced job crafting and encouraged them to set a job crafting goal. A month later the group came back together to share their experiences. Of the participants, 98 per cent reported that learning about job crafting was of personal and professional benefit and 80 per cent had been able to actively implement and achieve their job crafting goal. There were a number of other beneficial outcomes including increases in job satisfaction (+34 per cent) and enjoyment (+20 per cent) when pre- and post-intervention measures were compared.

As a consequence of the pilot and further feedback collected from participants, a decision was made to make job crafting workshops available across the CIO function. These were to be run not by external consultants, but by people from across the service who, having undergone job crafting training themselves, were able to contextualize the concept, draw from their personal experiences and share stories from colleagues across Virgin Money who had used job crafting to personalize their roles in beneficial ways.

Speaking to James, he explained that he was keen to introduce and test the concept of job crafting with colleagues within CIO for a number of reasons. First, job crafting enabled and encouraged people to weave experimentation and improvement into the fabric of their roles which aligned to the business need for driving innovation and improvement in 'smarter, more agile and less structured ways'. Second, a focus on harnessing individual strengths lifts perceptions about the business benefits that come from a diversity of thoughts, talents, experiences and backgrounds. James highlighted that, for example, from a neurodiversity perspective there is tremendous opportunity for people to apply atypical neurological, numerical and analytical talents within a data- and information-rich CIO function.

A third key benefit of job crafting from James' perspective as a business leader was that it enabled people to find, and check in with, the 'compass of their work' in terms of the value, purpose, direction and meaning of their jobs. Fourth, pragmatically, the concept was easy to adopt and apply; it wasn't, as James said, 'something you needed to carefully study and get a certificate in', it was something that could be directly and easily applied following the workshop sessions. Lastly, and just as importantly, James feels that personalizing work is just the right thing to do on a human level: 'Life's too short; if you hate or dislike something, just change it.'

Notes

1   Wrzesniewski, A (2014) Engage in job crafting, in J E Dutto and G M Spreitzer, *How to be a Positive Leader: Small actions, big impact*, Berrett-Koehler Publishers

2   Rudolph, C W *et al* (2017) Job crafting: a meta-analysis of relationships with individual differences, job characteristics, and work outcomes, *Journal of Vocational Behavior*, 102, pp 112–38

3   Lichtenthaler, P W and Fischbach, A (2016) Job crafting and motivation to continue working beyond retirement age, *Career Development International*, 21 (5), pp 477–97

4   Cheng, J C *et al* (2016) Tour leaders' job crafting and job outcomes: the moderating role of perceived organizational support, *Tourism Management Perspectives*, 20, pp 19–29

5   Rudolph, C W *et al* (2017) (see note 2 above)

6   Lichtenthaler, P W and Fischbach, A (2016) (see note 3 above)

7   Cheng, J C *et al* (2016) (see note 4 above)

8   Rudolph, C W *et al* (2017) (see note 2 above)

9   Lichtenthaler, P W and Fischbach, A (2016) (see note 3 above)

10 Slemp, G R and Vella-Brodrick, D A (2013) The Job Crafting Questionnaire: a new scale to measure the extent to which employees engage in job crafting, *International Journal of Wellbeing*, 3 (2), pp 126–46, doi:10.5502/ijw.v3i2.1

11 Cheng, J C and Yi, O (2018) Hotel employee job crafting, burnout, and satisfaction: the moderating role of perceived organizational support, *International Journal of Hospitality Management*, 72, pp 78–85

12 Tims, M, Bakker, A B and Derks, D (2013) The impact of job crafting on job demands, job resources, and well-being, *Journal of Occupational Health Psychology*, 18 (2), p 230

13 Rudolph, C W *et al* (2017) (see note 2 above)

14 Kim, M and Beehr, T A (2018) Can empowering leaders affect subordinates' well-being and careers because they encourage subordinates' job crafting behaviors? *Journal of Leadership & Organizational Studies*, 25 (2), pp 184–96

15 Terkel, S (2011) *Working: People talk about what they do all day and how they feel about what they do*, The New Press

16 Zhang, F and Parker, S K (2019) Reorienting job crafting research: a hierarchical structure of job crafting concepts and integrative review, *Journal of Organizational Behavior*, **40** (2), pp 126–46

17 Berg, J M, Dutton, J E and Wrzesniewski, A (2008) What is job crafting and why does it matter, available at https://positiveorgs.bus.umich.edu/wp-content/uploads/What-is-Job-Crafting-and-Why-Does-it-Matter1.pdf (archived at https://perma.cc/DQ77-4Z63). Retrieved 15 April 2011

18 Petrou, P *et al* (2012) Crafting a job on a daily basis: contextual correlates and the link to work engagement, *Journal of Organizational Behavior*, **33** (8), pp 1120–41

19 Ibid

20 Brenninkmeijer, V and Hekkert-Koning, M (2015) To craft or not to craft: the relationships between regulatory focus, job crafting and work outcomes, *Career Development International*, **20** (2), pp 147–62

21 Akkermans, J and Tims, M (2017) Crafting your career: how career competencies relate to career success via job crafting, *Applied Psychology*, **66** (1), pp 168–95

22 Kim, M and Beehr, T A (2018) (see note 14 above)

23 Cenciotti, R, Alessandri, G and Borgogni, L (2017) Psychological capital and career success over time: the mediating role of job crafting, *Journal of Leadership & Organizational Studies*, **24** (3), pp 372–84

24 Leana, C, Appelbaum, E and Shevchuk, I (2009) Work process and quality of care in early childhood education: the role of job crafting, *Academy of Management Journal*, **52** (6), pp 1169–92

25 Bacaksiz, F E, Tuna, R and Seren, A K H (2017) The relationships between organisational identification, job performance, and job crafting: a study among nurses, *International Journal of Caring Sciences*, **10** (1), p 251

26 Yepes-Baldó, M *et al* (2018) Job crafting, employee well-being, and quality of care, *Western Journal of Nursing Research*, **40**, pp 52–66, doi:10.1177/0193945916680614

27 Bakker, A B and Bal, M P (2010) Weekly work engagement and performance: a study among starting teachers, *Journal of Occupational and Organizational Psychology*, **83** (1), pp 189–206

28 Grant, A M (2007) Impact and the art of motivation maintenance: the effects of contact with beneficiaries on persistence behavior, *Organizational Behavior and Human Decision Processes*, **103** (1), pp 53–67

29 Ghitulescu, B E (2007) Shaping tasks and relationships at work: examining the antecedents and consequences of employee job crafting (Doctoral dissertation, University of Pittsburgh)

30 Tims, M, Bakker, A B and Derks, D (2015) Job crafting and job performance: a longitudinal study, *European Journal of Work and Organizational Psychology*, **24** (6), pp 914–28

31 Wrzesniewski, A (2014) (see note 1 above)

32 Lee, J Y and Lee, Y (2018) Job crafting and performance: literature review and implications for human resource development, *Human Resource Development Review*, **17** (3), pp 277–313

33 Oprea, B T *et al* (2019) Effectiveness of job crafting interventions: a meta-analysis and utility analysis, *European Journal of Work and Organizational Psychology*, **28** (6), pp 723–41

34 Petrou, P *et al* (2012) (see note 18 above)

35 Bindl, U K *et al* (2018) Job crafting revisited: implications of an extended framework for active changes at work, *Journal of Applied Psychology*, **104** (5), pp 605–28

36 Mattarelli, E and Tagliaventi, M R (2015) How offshore professionals' job dissatisfaction can promote further offshoring: organizational outcomes of job crafting, *Journal of Management Studies*, **52** (5), pp 585–620

37 Bindl, U K *et al* (2018) (see note 35 above)

38 Ibid

39 Mattarelli, E and Tagliaventi, M R (2015) (see note 36 above)

40 Siddiqi, M A (2015) Work engagement and job crafting of service employees influencing customer outcomes, *Vikalpa*, **40** (3), pp 277–92

41 Petrou, P, Demerouti, E and Schaufeli, W (2018) Crafting the change: the role of employee job crafting behaviors for successful organizational change, *Journal of Management*, **44**, pp 1766–92

42 Lichtenthaler, P W and Fischbach, A (2019) A meta-analysis on promotion- and prevention-focused job crafting, *European Journal of Work and Organizational Psychology*, **28** (1), pp 30–50

43 Lee, J Y and Lee, Y (2018) (see note 32 above)

44 Lichtenthaler, P W and Fischbach, A (2019) (see note 42 above)

45 Web of Science for education, available at: https://wok.mimas.ac.uk/ (archived at https://perma.cc/4AS7-Y3QY)

46 Petrou, P, Demerouti, E and Schaufeli, W B (2015) Job crafting in changing organizations: antecedents and implications for exhaustion and performance, *Journal of Occupational Health Psychology*, **20** (4), p 470

47 Tims, M, Bakker, A B and Derks, D (2013) (see note 12 above)

48 Petrou, P, Demerouti, E and Schaufeli, W B (2015) (see note 46 above)

49 Bindl, U K *et al* (2018) (see note 35 above)

50 Parker, S K, Wang, Y and Liao, J (2019) When is proactivity wise? A review of factors that influence the individual outcomes of proactive behavior, *Annual Review of Organizational Psychology and Organizational Behavior*, **6**, pp 221–48

51 Parker, S (2019) Proactive staff are great, but their efforts can backfire, Australian HR Institute, available at: https://www.hrmonline.com.au/research/proactivity-backfire/ (archived at https://perma.cc/JZ6R-UBSZ)

PART TWO

Experiment

05

Different forms of job crafting

Like people, job crafting comes in different shapes and sizes. It applies to all aspects of our work – our tasks, our relationships and how we think about work. As well as different types of job crafting, there are diverse motivations and ways that it can be applied, ranging from growth-oriented and generative crafting focused on building and improving tasks and relationships, to prevention-oriented and protective types of crafting which are often undertaken to reduce and narrow activities and overall job demands. Pulling from research, published case studies and practitioner experiences, this chapter will explore different types and directions of job crafting and the strengths and limitations of each approach.

Different types of job crafting

We will explore five different types of job crafting in this chapter. These are outlined in Figure 5.1 and can be thought of as the 'What' of job crafting. This is the middle section of the job crafting model which was introduced in Chapter 3.

Task crafting

Most jobs involve a series of tasks and activities. Task crafting is focused on making adjustments to these component parts and can be defined as proactively making tangible changes to aspects of a job including redesigning, adding or removing tasks, or reallocating time spent on different activities. If you think about your job as a series of building blocks that are stacked together to build a 'whole job', task crafting is focused on changing the shape, size and

FIGURE 5.1   Different types of crafting

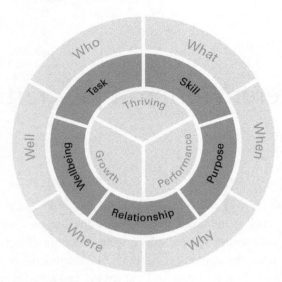

even colour and structure of these blocks. Task crafting is a foundational aspect of job crafting and is often combined with other types of crafting, recognizing that changing relational or development aspects of a role often shapes and impacts the tasks and activities in some way.

There are myriad ways to task craft, but there are four primary methods and common themes:

1 **Adding tasks:** employees can add additional tasks or activities that they find meaningful, stimulating or engaging into their jobs. For example, an HR officer with an interest in technology might add the task of using Twitter to send tweets about new policies, initiatives or training courses. Making this addition would enable the HR officer to experiment with new and different forms of connection with their colleagues across the organization and track interest and engagement for particular tweets. It would also provide a new channel to engage with the wider workforce which could, for example, enable people to raise issues or queries with the HR team.

2 **Emphasizing activities:** people can invest in tasks that they see as particularly enjoyable and meaningful that are already part of their jobs by giving them more time, energy and focus. For example, an IT technician with a keen interest in customer service could actively volunteer to be a first point of contact for a specific service area or become the go-to guy for queries relating to specific software applications.

3 **Redesigning tasks:** redesigning tasks refers to doing existing tasks in a new way. When time constraints make adding or emphasizing tasks more problematic, employees can find ways to change and shape existing activities to make them more meaningful and interesting.[1] For example, rather than simply relying on email as a form of communication, people could make an effort to pick up the phone or meet with someone in person. Another example might include using new software or new processes to deliver services they have done in the past. In terms of team communication this could include experimenting with new online messaging such as Slack, Microsoft Teams or Rocket Chat.

4 **Removing and reducing tasks:** people can craft their role by removing or reducing certain tasks that they undertake or by simplifying them and making them less intense and taxing. An example of this could be a cook reducing the items on the menu, an entrepreneur paying for an accountant to manage their finances and book keeping, a manager cancelling or reducing the time commitment of non-essential meetings, or a project director delegating bid writing to colleagues. Removing tasks always needs to be done with care to ensure that the wider implications of not doing any work are known and understood, or in the case of delegating, people are not simply 'dumping' their work on others.

EXAMPLE
Task crafting

Paul worked in the IT department and had a passion for testing, and trying to crash, new software before it was released across the organization. He loved trying to spot bugs in systems. He did this testing in his 'spare time' at work, over lunch and staying late.

Over time, his passion and expertise for this work started to be recognized. Colleagues approached Paul to test their software before a wider release. Through discussions with his manager, Paul added this responsibility into his job role and now spends approximately half a day every two weeks testing new software. Paul gets the opportunity to do something he loves, and the organization benefits from Paul's passion and expertise.

Skill crafting

Individuals have a unique insight into themselves and the requirements of their own jobs. Skill crafting enables people to shape their personal development in ways that are most beneficial to them personally, which ultimately positively impacts on the work they do. Skill crafting can be defined as making changes to a job that are linked to growing and refining specialist and practical skills, knowledge and expertise. Skill crafting does not always have to include developing new skills, but could include refining and consolidating existing knowledge and expertise.

Skill crafting includes learning that is structured, work-based or self-directed as well as wider professional development activities. Structured learning would include activities such as taking an external training course or qualifications. Work-based learning could include volunteering for specific projects, shadowing a colleague to learn a specific skill, or taking on new responsibilities. Self-directed learning could include reading specific papers or articles, or joining a specialist online group or forum. Lastly, professional development would include activities such as training or mentoring others, joining professional bodies or networking with others.

There are three key ways in which people can skill craft:

1 **Growing new skills and knowledge.** This type of crafting is focused on seeking out, developing and growing new skills and knowledge related to work. This could include developing wider capabilities, trying to learn new things that go beyond core skills, and pursuing opportunities for extending overall knowledge. For example, someone could volunteer for a new project, a software engineer could learn and experiment with a new programming language, a finance manager could learn about the application of artificial intelligence and machine learning for their service, or a new line manager could take a programme focused on building and developing leadership skills.

2 **Consolidating and protecting skills and knowledge.** This element of crafting involves creating and finding opportunities to consolidate and deepen existing knowledge and expertise and proactively shaping work to ensure that skills and knowledge are not lost. This could include channelling efforts towards maintaining a specific area of expertise and actively staying on top of knowledge in relation to core areas of a job. For example, an HR manager could volunteer to chair or lead certain employee relations cases for their organization despite the fact that this is not a primary or core

part of their role. This enables them to consolidate their existing knowledge and expertise and additionally gives them an incentive to keep up to date with organizational policies and employment case law.

3 **Redesigning existing tasks to develop skills and knowledge.** This type of skill crafting relates to knowledge and skills which are developed through redesigning the way existing tasks are undertaken. Some examples could include a team leader learning about and exploring the use of collaborative software, such as Google Docs, Dropbox or Microsoft SharePoint, to build and edit new documents and track projects; a manager could experiment with different formats of meeting styles, such as having daily standups, walking meetings, silent meetings or even cancelling existing meetings altogether.

EXAMPLE
Skill crafting

Adeline is an organizational development manager at a law firm. She is keen to experiment with using Agile approaches and methodologies to design and shape future training courses. To date, the majority of courses she has developed and commissioned have been designed with input primarily from senior leaders and consultants and often the sessions have been 'rolled out' on an organizational basis without being tested with or tweaked for specific audiences.

To learn more about Agile, Adeline does some reading about the concept and then engages with some online research and resources. She consolidates this knowledge by shadowing colleagues from their IT team who use Agile approaches and she participates in a number of sprints to understand the approach. Adeline has skill crafted by deliberately and actively growing her knowledge about Agile ways of working.

Adeline experiments with an Agile approach in response to a request to design and run a training course for first-time team leaders. She decides that rather than curate or commission a standalone course, she will hold a series of short sprints involving existing and new line managers to design an outline and content for the training course. The outcome of this new approach is a pilot session which will be tested with a small number of colleagues. Rather than being a traditional 'lecture style' training session, based on feedback and ideas from the group the proposed session is much more interactive and the content comes from existing managers rather than relying on external speakers.

Relationship crafting

Relationship or relational crafting involves people shaping or changing the nature of their connections, relationships and interactions with others in their work. This could include actively seeking to meet new people, deepening existing relationships, and creating opportunities for greater interaction and collaboration. As well as building relationships, relational crafting can be used to 'dial down' interactions with other people. This could include deliberately avoiding or spending less time with specific individuals or more broadly minimizing aspects of the job that involve socializing or connecting with other people.

From a broad array of research, we know that high-quality connections can have a number of positive benefits including adaptability in jobs and overall careers,[2] increased satisfaction[3] and overall physiological functioning.[4] Relationships and connections with others are a powerful way in which to influence an individual's performance, wellbeing and sense of meaning in their work.

People generally relationship craft in one of three different ways:

1 **Building and amplifying relationships.** Employees can build satisfaction and meaning by creating new, and amplifying existing, relationships with others who enable them to feel a sense of fun, dignity, confidence and worth. For example, I've known people schedule lunch dates with their work friends to ensure that they spend quality time together. Other examples include people asking others to mentor them, collaborating with and shadowing others, or simply finding more opportunities for team members to informally connect.

2 **Reframing relationships.** People can change how they frame established relationships to foster better connections and minimize or ameliorate difficult and problematic relationships. For example, in a situation where a person always appears to object to or block your ideas for service improvements, it would be easy to get frustrated and even take the issue personally. One way to reframe this relationship would be to explore what other explanations might exist for the person challenging your ideas – they might, for instance, be particularly risk averse or they may be overplaying a strength of prudence or protection. Rather than being critical of you, they may simply be trying to protect the team or organization by keeping the status quo.

3 **Adapting relationships.** By broadening and adapting existing work relationships people can find new ways to connect with others and more opportunities to act in ways that are purposeful and meaningful. For example, someone could deliberately try to make an effort to understand

more about the hobbies, passions and interests of a colleague – giving them something to talk about and demonstrating a care for the individual that goes beyond work. Another example might include a more experienced employee adapting relationships with new starters to focus on mentoring or coaching, which could be meaningful and beneficial for both the mentor and mentee. I've also seen people adapt and broaden relationships by starting or joining groups such as book clubs.

EXAMPLE
Relationship crafting

As an Executive Director, Joanne had an extremely challenging role. Over time she felt that opportunities for her to connect with her team were reducing. Whilst she spent a lot of time in the presence of others in – often back-to-back – meetings, there were precious few opportunities to genuinely connect with people. It was often easier and quicker to get things down by email rather than having a person-to-person conversation. But this did not reflect Joanne's personal style or work preference. Joanne made a micro job crafting goal that once a day she would attempt to either phone or speak face to face with one of the team members rather than sending an email. This 'cost' her 10–15 minutes a day but Joanne said it made a big difference to her work. Through this new habit she was taking back some control in how she worked, with greater alignment to her working preferences and beliefs.

Purpose crafting

Purpose crafting, or cognitive crafting, refers to reframing how we think about our work. This includes spending time reflecting on the value and significance of our work individually and for others, including our friends and family and our customers and colleagues. Often this encourages us to think about our work as a whole rather than separate tasks and exploring how the work we do fulfils meaningful personal, organizational or wider societal goals. It could also involve focusing on and thinking about the best parts of the job or aspects of work that are most meaningful. There are three primary ways that people tend to purpose craft:

1 **Promoting purpose.** Individuals can foster a sense of purpose and meaning by broadening their perceptions of the impact and significance of their jobs for other people. This can involve reflecting on work as a whole,

rather than as a number of standalone activities and connections. For example, rather than seeing their work as stacking bookshelves, ordering books and dealing with individual customers, someone working in a public library could see the purpose of their work as the ability to share and provide access to both information and knowledge at the same time as promoting a sense of local community. A study of zookeepers[5] found that rather than seeing their work as being arduous, involving cleaning enclosures and feeding animals – which represented the majority of their job roles – they reported their work in a much broader sense, including a moral duty to nurture, protect and care for animals.

2 **Narrowing purpose.** We can create a sense of purpose by focusing in on and recognizing specific elements of work which we find particularly meaningful and enjoyable. In contrast to expanding perceptions, this involves narrowing the mental scope of the purpose of a job to specific tasks, skills and relationships. This approach may be most useful for people who don't enjoy elements of their work, but do find other specific parts of their jobs to be meaningful and engaging. For example, someone working on customer services could focus on reflecting on the customers they helped the most. Or if someone enjoys problem solving, they could focus on the aspects of their job that help them solve problems for their customers.

3 **Connecting with purpose.** People can craft cognitively by connecting elements of the work they do with the passions and interests that are important to them, which may traditionally only be displayed and showcased outside of work. For example, someone with a passion for running could start a running group at work, which helps others get fit, builds relationships with others, and creates a regular opportunity to get outside.

EXAMPLE
Purpose crafting

Lucy worked in a customer service centre for a bank. Her days were hectic and spent mostly speaking and interacting with customers, with little time or ability to change her day-to-day tasks. So she decided to get creative about shaping her work following a job crafting workshop. Lucy decided to commit five minutes each evening to reflecting on the customers she helped the most. In the morning she left a diary on the seat of her car. She set this goal because it was important to Lucy that she was helping others through the work she did. Before driving home each evening, she made a note of the day's most positive customer experience. After a month she had over 20 examples of how she was making a difference to customers' lives.

Wellbeing crafting

Wellbeing crafting involves proactively shaping how work is done to positively influence overall levels of wellbeing. This includes making changes to work that promote mental and physical health and changing aspects of work and routines which might be having a detrimental impact. There are three key ways that people tend to wellbeing craft:

1 **Promoting wellbeing.** People can promote their wellbeing by finding and introducing new ways to be more active, recharged, absorbed and engaged at work. This might include taking more deliberate and regular breaks to refresh, using lunch breaks to get some exercise, practising mindfulness during the day, taking naps or making more nutritious snacks rather than eating calorific treats from the local sandwich shop.

2 **Limiting stress and strain.** This type of wellbeing crafting involves finding ways to minimize or prevent aspects of work that an individual has identified as a source of negative stress and strain. Some examples could include, stopping checking emails in the evening or at the weekend, saying no to non-critical work requests, getting into the routine of leaving the office 'on time' (whatever that means for the individual) and directly seeking support to address a negative relationship.

3 **Redesigning tasks to bring wellbeing.** This involves redesigning existing ways of working to foster health and wellbeing further. For example, taking the stairs rather than the lift once a day, having walking 1-to-1 meetings, banning cakes and biscuits as a team for a month or using a standing desk for parts of the day.

EXAMPLE
Wellbeing crafting

Ali recognizes that he finds it increasingly difficult to concentrate at work. He gets easily distracted by the pings and pongs he receives from his computers and phone alerting him to new emails arriving, new posts on social media, or another WhatsApp message. He is also interested in the concept of mindfulness and learning more about ways of improving his focus and attention. Ali decides to craft his work in a number of ways. First, he turns off all notifications on his phone and desktop computer. Second, he schedules batches of regular times during the day when he will check his phone and email. Third, at lunchtime, three times a week, he finds a quiet space to sit (outside ideally if it is sunny) and listens to a mindfulness app. These changes not only bring Ali greater focus in his work but they have other unintended consequences too. He finds he gets a positive sense of achievement from successfully making positive changes to the way he does his job and he enjoys the sense of calm and focus he feels after the mindfulness sessions.

Different job crafting drivers and directions

A primary power of job crafting is that it enables people to craft in different directions depending on their personal needs and motivations. When exploring job crafting with groups and individuals, as well as explaining the different types and subsets of job crafting, I share the three different ways or directions that people tend to craft. These are shown in Figure 5.2 and are summarized below.

FIGURE 5.2 Different directions and drivers for job crafting

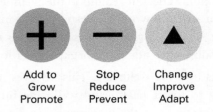

Three key different directions and drivers for job crafting are:

1 **Growth focus – Add, Grow, Promote.** This way of crafting is focused on adding, growing and promoting tasks, relationships, skills, purpose and wellbeing within the existing job. This primarily involves expanding elements of the job to incorporate new ways of working.

2 **Avoidance focus – Stop, Reduce, Prevent.** Avoidance crafting involves proactively protecting, limiting or moving away from negative aspects of work which might relate to specific tasks or relationships or more broadly overall negative stresses, strains and challenges of work.

3 **Redesign focus – Change, Improve, Adapt.** Rather than adding or taking away aspects of a job, crafting with a redesign focus involves actively changing, improving or adapting existing ways of working, thinking and interacting.

Table 5.1 provides a summary of both the different types and the different focuses of job crafting.

TABLE 5.1 A summary of different job crafting approaches

Type of job crafting	Definition	Approach crafting: *adding, growing, promoting*	Avoidance crafting: *stopping, reducing, preventing*	Change crafting: *improving, adapting, redesigning*
Task crafting	Shaping the number, type and nature of tasks and activities.	Adding, growing and developing existing tasks and activities.	Stopping, removing, or protecting specific tasks and activities.	Redesigning how existing tasks are performed or delivering agreed outcomes using different approaches.
Skill crafting	Creating opportunities to grow, develop and consolidate skills and knowledge.	Developing new skills and knowledge related to new activities and projects.	Deepening, consolidating, or finding ways to focus on existing skills and knowledge.	Developing new skills, knowledge and approaches to deliver existing tasks and activities.
Relationship crafting	Changing the nature of relationships and interactions with people at work.	Building new relationships at work by seeking and developing opportunities to meet and interact with others.	Deepening relationships or limiting and restricting interactions with certain individuals or groups.	Adapting, broadening and reframing existing relationships with individuals and groups.
Purpose crafting	Shaping thoughts and perceptions of the value, meaning and purpose of work.	Focusing and thinking about work as a whole rather than separate tasks, and thinking about the broader impact and meaning.	Reflecting on and identifying specific elements of work that are meaningful and enjoyable.	Making connections between work and personal passions and interests to foster meaning, interest and engagement.

(continued)

TABLE 5.1 (Continued)

Type of job crafting	Definition	Approach crafting: *adding, growing, promoting*	Avoidance crafting: *stopping, reducing, preventing*	Change crafting: *improving, adapting, redesigning*
Wellbeing crafting	Crafting work in ways that positively influence an individual's health and wellbeing.	Introducing new ways of working and work routines that positively influence health and wellbeing.	Minimizing or restricting aspects of work that are negative sources of stress such as unwelcome and uncontrollable challenges and job demands.	Performing existing tasks, activities and working routines in ways that positively influence health and wellbeing.

Are some directions of job crafting better than others?

The question of whether one direction or focus of job crafting is better than any other is interesting. Broadly, the beneficial aspects of job crafting are often most strongly associated with growth activities, involving individuals proactively shaping, amplifying and building aspects of their jobs both physically and cognitively. Fundamentally, this type of crafting (often referred to as approach crafting) enables people to shape their work in positive ways.

To date, the evidence for contraction- and avoidance-focused job crafting is more mixed. On the face of it, job crafting in ways that minimize or reduce the demands of the job seems like it should be an effective strategy to cope with excessive and challenging workloads. However, empirical studies have shown that this is not always the case. In fact, job crafting which reduces the demands of a role or is designed to escape or move away from negative aspects of the job has been negatively related to work engagement and job satisfaction.[6] Other studies have shown that avoidance job crafting has been linked to exhaustion. So, paradoxically, people who try to cope with the stresses and demands of their job by reducing, minimizing or stopping certain aspects of their job may actually find themselves more exhausted and less engaged and satisfied as a consequence.

There are a number of reasons that might explain the weaker and, at times, negative association between avoidance crafting and measures such as engagement and satisfaction. First, the negative relationship could be because crafting of this nature is focused on alleviating or dealing with a hindering or negative aspect of work. Making small changes to deal with suboptimal aspects of a job might be a useful first step, but it may not be sufficient to tip the balance into making the job particularly satisfying and engaging overall. Similarly, the changes might not be enough to address specific low levels of wellbeing or happiness. For example, starting to take regular breaks during the day may be helpful restoratively but will do little to address overall high workload levels. Second, avoidance crafting includes changes that are often not openly celebrated or encouraged. Consequently, people may also be more reticent to admit to their colleagues and their line managers in particular that they are struggling with certain aspects of their job. Employees may therefore feel guilty that they are unable to meet their targets, or uncomfortable with disclosing that they are finding certain relationships difficult and tricky. Third, some researchers have argued[7] that removing certain tasks or reducing overall work levels may, unintentionally, make the work less stimulating, which could influence people's satisfaction with their work.

SHOULD AVOIDANCE- AND PREVENTION-ORIENTED CRAFTING BE AVOIDED ALTOGETHER?

So, on balance, should the advice be to avoid job crafting activities that have a focus on reducing or narrowing activities and interactions that promote safety and minimize risk? Should prevention-oriented crafting of this nature be considered negative and counterproductive? I don't think so.

Crafting with a prevention focus enables individuals to understand and deal with aspects of the work that are hindering them and allows them to focus their actions and thoughts in ways which manage these limitations. This can be an important first step in making the job more manageable, lead to achievable change in the longer term, and it provides a platform for people to craft more positive elements into their work.

My thoughts on prevention-oriented crafting have been shaped by conversations with Dr Uta Bindl, a work psychology, human resources and job crafting scholar. Together with colleagues,[8] Dr Bindl has investigated the efficacy and impact of different types of job crafting. Whilst in her studies she has found that promotion-oriented activities involving shaping, seeking and building aspects of jobs tended to be more strongly associated with creativity and innovation, she does not feel that avoidance and prevention-oriented methods of crafting should be discouraged. Dr Bindl believes it would be a mistake to dismiss prevention-focused job crafting out of hand. Crafting in ways which protect the individual, reduce their demands, address poor relationships or channel focus and attention is useful and meaningful. But making these types of changes might be more complicated for employees to do with confidence and in a way that doesn't put off their managers and co-workers. As Dr Bindl told me:

> Prevention-oriented job crafting is important because it might be the most appropriate way to meet and address the immediate needs of an individual in being able to perform their job, but unfortunately it might also be the type of crafting that gets more pushback and challenge from line managers.

Rather than prevention-focused crafting being negative itself, it might instead be the perceptions and associated feelings of this type of behaviour that explain the more complicated and nuanced relationships of this type of crafting with factors such as engagement, satisfaction and wellbeing. For example, a computer programmer could craft their job to ensure that they left work 'on time' at least three times a week, recognizing that consistently staying late at work or working in the evenings is having an overall negative impact on their health, motivation and energy levels both at home and life in general. However, other colleagues who are also staying late to manage workloads could view this crafting behaviour as negative, putting more pressure on them to cover. Similarly, a team leader could see this as a sign of a lack of commitment. Consequently, the employee may feel guilty about crafting in this way, which reduces their satisfaction and engagement. The context and support in which prevention-oriented crafting is undertaken and the feelings and perceptions of the employee and their co-workers and managers need to be considered. Dr Bindl believes more research is needed to explore and understand these further.

Conclusion

There are rich and diverse ways in which people can craft and personalize their working behaviours and experiences. Whilst there are five distinct forms of job crafting (task, relationship, purpose, wellbeing and skill), in practice these often overlap and complement each other. Job crafting can be used to grow, reduce or change different elements of work.

The direction and focus of an employee's job crafting efforts will be influenced by internal and external factors including their motivations, circumstances, passions, the freedom and autonomy they experience in their role and the culture and the environment they work in.

The manner and motivation with which people craft ends up being as unique as the people doing the crafting.

The secret to setting effective job crafting goals and making job crafting more effective and beneficial is to recognize and work with, rather than against, the organizational context in which an employee is working. The next chapter will explore a framework and approach for establishing compelling job crafting goals in ways that are most likely to have a sustainable impact for the individual and their organization.

KEY POINTS

- There are five key types of job crafting – task crafting, skill crafting, relationship crafting, wellbeing crafting and purpose crafting.

- In practice, when people job craft they often do a number of different types of crafting at the same time.

- There are three different orientations and directions in which job crafting can be performed – growth focus, avoidance focus and redesign focus.

- Each different direction and orientation of job crafting has strengths and limitations – broadly there is more research support showing the benefits of growth and approach crafting.

KEY QUESTIONS

- Are there any types of job crafting that seem more relevant to you, or your organization, than others?

- How openly would you, or leaders in your organization, support and encourage avoidance-oriented job crafting?

- What capacity do you see people in your organization having to try to experiment with new ways of working?

- How often are people encouraged to reflect on how they do their work?

CASE STUDY
Crafting magic in the clouds with Widerøe

Widerøe is the largest regional airline in Scandinavia. The company flies around 3 million passengers annually and has a staff of over 3,000 people. One of the strong underlying beliefs at Widerøe is to 'be personal', not only in how they treat customers, but also in how colleagues bring themselves to their job.

As Chief Cabin Instructor Siv Heidi Breivik explained to me, Widerøe actively encourages colleagues to use themselves, their experiences and resources to craft the way in which they interact with passengers and co-workers. Cabin crew training is rigorous and intense, with a tremendous amount of information that new flight attendants need to learn and be comfortable with to support the safety, security and comfort of their passengers. But in addition to the mandatory training which would be commonplace in any airline, Widerøe encourages crew members to reflect on how they can bring their personal strengths and passions to their jobs and what kind of positive impact they want to have on their passengers and the crews they work with.

The work of a flight attendant is busy and demanding. But aspects of the work can be repetitive and routine too – doing the same flights and the same routine procedures hundreds of times every month. Widerøe encourages attendants to job craft in order to both break up the repetitive nature of their jobs and to do their work in personally meaningful ways which enable their strengths and personalities to shine. As Siv explained to me:

> You can make magic with passengers and your colleagues by doing your work in meaningful ways... but you have to experiment and find your own way to do this.

Siv believes that flight attendants have the opportunity to see their roles as conductors, with the power and opportunity to influence and shape the mood of passengers during their flight. Small actions and demonstrations of empathy have the potential to change the mood of not only one passenger but the whole flight. Discretionary acts of kindness, such as cleaning the smudged glasses of a small child, or putting a blanket on a sleeping passenger, signals care and compassion, not only to the recipient of the act but those around them. Similarly, dealing with frustrated or upset customers provides opportunities for crew members to demonstrate empathy and understanding as well as problem solving and creativity. These actions have the potential to create positive waves which Siv says you can see ripple through the plane in how other passengers interact with each other.

Cabin Instructor Lasse Kvarsnes Hansen says that one of the positive and distinctive aspects of Widerøe is that they encourage people to find ways to task craft their work that bring their personal selves to their routine activities. For example, attendants are trusted to create their own personal style for pre-flight briefings and flight announcements; most airlines or organizations don't provide this freedom. Similarly, Lasse explains that attendants can use relational job crafting to make connections with other passengers or colleagues during the flight. This could include seeking out opportunities to engage with younger or elderly passengers if this is something that an attendant particularly cares about.

Cecilie Torset, Cabin Instructor and Cabin Crew member, shared other examples of how she crafts her role, and encourages others to do the same. She explained to me:

> Passengers often have a lot of baggage that they bring on board and not just suitcases and luggage... as a cabin crew member you have the opportunity to learn about others, share stories and support people.

Cecilie actively tries to relationship craft and build relationships from the moment people step onto the plane:

> When passengers step on board, you have an opportunity to welcome them, but also to connect and show that you really see and recognize them as an individual. I greet people warmly in a way that invites them to respond back and then build on this first connection throughout the flight.

When training others, Cecilie encourages crew members to find their own personal ways of making and creating 'the best day ever' for themselves and their passengers. She finds that crew members are most able to craft and shape their work once they have settled into their roles, the flight protocols and procedures have become routine and crew members have the mental space to think about how they can adapt and customize their approach.

Widerøe create opportunities for cabin crew to craft their role on the ground as well as in the skies. Siv explains that the background and experiences of Widerøe's flight attendants are incredibly rich and diverse and that people are encouraged to explore and find ways to bring their expertise and interests to their role. For example, there are a number of trained nurses who have retrained as flight attendants, and they contribute to and support the first-aid training that the company delivers.

Job crafting, Lasse says, 'gives you and the passengers something extra'. Siv and Cecilie all agree with Lasse that shaping work in personally meaningful ways can bring a spark to it. Job crafting has the power to create moments of magic during a flight – which can connect crew and customers in wonderful ways.

Notes

1   Berg, J M, Dutton, J E and Wrzesniewski, A (2013) Job crafting and meaningful work, in (eds) B J Dik, Z S Byrne and M F Steger, *Purpose and Meaning in the Workplace* (pp 81–104), Washington, DC: American Psychological Association

2   Dutton, J E (2003) *Energize Your Workplace: How to create and sustain high-quality connections at work*, San Francisco: Jossey-Bass

3   Dutton, J E and Heaphy, E D (2003) The power of high-quality connections, in (eds) K S Cameron, J E Dutton and R E Quinn, *Positive Organizational Scholarship: Foundations of a new discipline* (pp 263–78), San Francisco: Berrett-Koehler

4   Seligman, M E (2012) *Flourish: A visionary new understanding of happiness and well-being*, Simon and Schuster

5   Bunderson, J S and Thompson, J.A (2009) The call of the wild: zookeepers, callings, and the double-edged sword of deeply meaningful work, *Administrative Science Quarterly*, 54, pp 32–57

6   Rudolph, C et al (2017) Job crafting: a meta-analysis of relationships with individual differences, job characteristics, and work outcomes, *Journal of Vocational Behavior*, 102, pp 112–38 https://doi.org/10.1016/j.jvb.2017.05.008 (archived at https://perma.cc/7KP6-XYCQ)

7   Petrou, P et al (2012) Crafting a job on a daily basis: contextual correlates and the link to work engagement, *Journal of Organizational Behavior*, 33 (8), pp 1120–41

8   Bindl, U K et al (2019) Job crafting revisited: implications of an extended framework for active changes at work, *Journal of Applied Psychology*, 104 (5), pp 605–28, ISSN 0021-9010

06

Setting job crafting goals

Whilst people often quickly grasp the idea of job crafting they frequently become unstuck when it comes to making it a reality. How do you, or your colleagues, find the opportunity to job craft when there are so many other competing demands, deadlines and priorities in your day-to-day work life? Making change of any kind happen is hard, irrespective of how motivated or committed we might be. This is particularly the case in complex, challenging and demanding work environments.

Fortunately, job crafting does not involve adding more hours to the day. Effective job crafting strategies might actually be the key to finding and unlocking both time and energy at work.

The secret to, and science of, making job crafting a sustainable habit and routine way of working is through creating small, regular, compelling actions that balance practicality and passion. The best way to ensure this is through a combination of planning and goal setting.

Asking the right questions

As any coach will tell you, the right questions are fundamental to enabling people to self-reflect and identify opportunities for change and experimentation. I find that when working with groups and individuals, themed questions can be useful to stimulate thought, energy and excitement about the areas of their work they want to personalize and craft further. There are six themes of questions that I find are particularly useful (see Figure 6.1). These represent the 'How' of job crafting and are the outer ring of the job crafting model shared in Chapter 3.

FIGURE 6.1   The how of job crafting

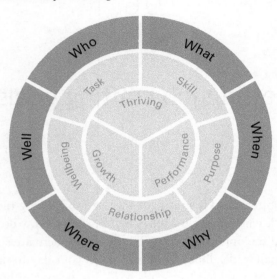

Well? How well do you feel at work?

At the heart of the 'Well?' question theme is understanding how work currently influences an individual's health and wellbeing and exploring the positive changes to the way work is carried out, thought about, or physically structured. Whilst the majority of job crafting goals in this theme relate to wellbeing crafting, there is often overlap with other job crafting areas as they frequently involve doing (task crafting) and thinking about work differently (purpose crafting), changing relationships (relationship crafting) and learning or sharing skills (skill crafting).

12 'WELL'-RELATED QUESTIONS

1 What aspects of your work positively/negatively influence your health and wellbeing?

2 What changes to your work would most positively influence your wellbeing?

3 What wellbeing initiatives at work can you involve yourself in, or contribute to?

4 What skills or knowledge could you develop to give you more confidence in being able to meet the challenges you face in your work?

5 How could you increase your physical activity in your working day?

6 What approaches do you use to manage and maintain your energy levels at work?

7 What opportunities do you currently take to recharge during the day?

8 How regularly do you take all the breaks you are entitled to?

9 How happy are you with the balance between your work and home life?

10 What approaches do you have to switch off at the end of the day? Do you have any ideas to do this better?

11 How healthily do you feel you eat and drink during the day? How could you be even healthier?

12 Do you have any personal skills or passions that you could share with colleagues? How could you do this?

Who? Who do you work with?

A second question theme is 'Who?' Exploring who people work with and the quality of their relationships at work enables and encourages people to identify opportunities to build, change or limit their relationships with others. The majority of job crafting goals identified through the exploration of these questions relate to relationship crafting.

12 'WHO'-RELATED QUESTIONS

1 Who are your key stakeholders?

2 How strong are your relationships?

3 Who do you have the greatest connections with?

4 Who do you enjoy working with the most/least?

5 Who do you find particularly helpful at work?

6 Who inspires you at work?

7 Who do you feel is a good role model at work?

8 Who do you provide support to in your role?

9 Who would you like to build stronger relationships with?

10 What are your most challenging and/or complex relationships at work?

11 Who does your work impact on (internal or external to the organization)?

12 How can you foster a greater sense of belonging amongst your colleagues?

What? What do you do?

The third question theme is 'What?' Questions around this theme are focused on the tasks and responsibilities of people's jobs, the aspects they love, the parts they dislike and the changes that they can make. Exploring questions of this nature often encourages task crafting.

12 'WHAT'-RELATED QUESTIONS

1 What aspects of your work do you enjoy the most?

2 What aspects of your work do you enjoy the least?

3 What are your strengths? How could you apply your strengths more at work?

4 What are your most important tasks and responsibilities?

5 What aspects of your work do you have most control over?

6 What aspects of your work do you have least control over?

7 What aspects of your work would you like to change?

8 What elements of your work could you do better?

9 What areas of your work could you stop doing, or do less of? What would happen if you did this?

10 What support or resources would most benefit you to be able to do your job better?

11 What opportunities are there to reduce the demands and challenges of your job?

12 If you could experiment with making one change to how you did your job, what would it be?

When? When do you work?

The fourth question theme is 'When?' Many, but certainly not all, jobs give people some flexibility in relation to when certain tasks or activities are done.

Our mental sharpness and motivational levels don't remain static – they fluctuate during the day. The rhythm and times at which our abilities peak and trough vary from person to person. Our individual circadian rhythms and correspondingly our alertness and energy levels may mean that we are better suited to performing different tasks at different times of the day.

Exploring and deliberately experimenting with when and how people approach the timing and design of their working day often gives rise to task crafting opportunities.

12 'WHEN'-RELATED QUESTIONS

1 When during the day do you find you have most energy at work?

2 When during the day do you find you have least energy at work?

3 When do you feel most refreshed during the week?

4 What tasks allow you flexibility over the frequency and/or time they are performed?

5 How do you plan the structure of your day?

6 How could you be more deliberate in planning or allocating time for different tasks and activities?

7 If you were to experiment with doing your work in a different order what would it be?

8 When do you currently take or schedule breaks and times for recovery during the day?

9 When do you get your best ideas?

10 If you could create your dream working hours what would they be?

11 When are the times of day that your customers/stakeholders value your attention?

12 When are the times of day that you are disturbed the most / least?

Why? Why do you work?

The fifth question theme is 'Why?' Asking why we do things helps gets to the heart of the purpose and value of the work we do and how it aligns to our personal beliefs. Questions of this nature often lead to cognitive or purpose crafting.

12 'WHY'-RELATED QUESTIONS

1 Why is your job important to you?

2 How do you describe your work to others?

3 How do your friends and family benefit from the work you do?

4 How does your job benefit the organization?

5 How does your job benefit other people inside and outside of the organization?

6 What is the purpose of your job?

7 How does your work provide value to others?

8 Which elements of your work do you personally feel are most important?

9 How does your work link to the wider purpose of the organization?

10 How could you reframe how you think and describe your work in ways that demonstrate the impact of your job on others?

11 How does your work align to your personal values?

12 What elements of your work are you most proud of?

Where? Where do you work?

The sixth and final question theme is 'Where?' The focus of these questions is to understand the different locations in which people currently work and the opportunities they have, and make, to work in different places either within, or outside, of their traditional working environment. Increasingly technology is making it easier to do all, or core, aspects of our work in different spaces.

Dr Cal Newport strongly believes that where we do and think about our work matters. Dr Newport is a computer scientist and author of books such as *Deep Work*,[1] on how and when people do their best work. He argues[2] that people should be deliberate in choosing where they do their work, because working in different locations enables people to break free from traditional work routines. In particular, he is an advocate of finding novel or interesting places to work because not only do they limit the amount of day-to-day office distractions, they can create visual and sensory stimulus to create new insights and thoughts. For example, working at your desk in an open-plan office with your phone switched on and emails only a click away may not be the best or most productive place to do focused work which involves deep thinking and concentration.

12 WHERE'-RELATED QUESTIONS

1 Where do you do your best thinking?

2 Where do you feel most energized?

3 Where do you do your most focused work?

4 Where do you have your best conversations and ideas with colleagues?

5 What opportunities do you have to work in different locations in your office?

6 What opportunities do you have to work from home or other external locations?

7 What tools do you use to connect with colleagues in ways that are not person to person?

8 If you were to experiment with working in a different work location where would it be?

9 If you needed to work with full concentration and no distraction what would be your dream location to work from? Who else would you have around?

10 If you wanted to generate and stimulate new ideas what would be your dream location to work from? Who else would you have around?

11 To what extent do you make the most of your opportunities to work flexibly?

12 What opportunities are there to do elements of your work physically outside?

Finding the right questions

The purpose of asking these exploratory questions is to enable and encourage people to think more deeply, deliberately and potentially differently about their work. Not all questions would be relevant and going through each of these themes in one go would be exhausting.

The questions can be explored individually or with a colleague or line manager, either individually or in groups. Of course, these questions are not exhaustive, and they should certainly be adapted to reflect individual circumstances and interests. I find it works well if people pick one specific theme at a time to explore and focus on. For example, a team interested in encouraging job crafting could pick a different theme and related questions to explore each month and then run different individual or group job crafting experiments to see if they can make tweaks and changes to their work to make it even better.

The relevance and resonance of the questions will depend on the individual and their role, but I have learnt not to make assumptions about what areas and themes are relevant. For example, when working with call centre staff I made the assumption that people had to work from a fixed office location at all times. However, it turned out that the organization I was working with offered people the flexibility to work from home or other locations to make calls. Additionally, the team had access to a variety of spaces in their offices for breaks, informal catch-ups and team meetings.

Creating compelling job crafting goals

Identifying ideas to make work better, meaningful and personal is only part of the process when it comes to job crafting. Ideas need to be turned into action. For many people it can be a challenge to translate ideas into reality, to manage mis-steps and distractions and to find the energy, enthusiasm and commitment to follow through with (the best) plans and intentions.

Why change is hard

Making change is hard. If it was easy, we would all be as fit, slim, rested and enlightened as we want to be. New Year's resolutions would have 100 per cent, rather than 40 per cent[3] success rates. At work, we would be able to achieve the goals we set ourselves and focus our attention, energies and behaviours on the things that matter most to us, whilst resisting distractions and temptations presented by others, or that sometimes we make for ourselves. Unfortunately, life is not like this. Our brains and lives are full of unhelpful habits and routines that are often difficult to break free from.

Change can often feel clumsy. Trying new ways of working, particularly breaking away from well-worn routines, often involves using techniques or approaches that we have not used before and consequently will need practice and refinement to get right. We will often make mistakes when starting something new, and at times this can make us feel uncertain and vulnerable.

One of the best descriptions of the inherent 'bumpiness' of trying new things was shared by a senior leader working in the Civil Service. He had wanted to change the way that he started meetings with his team. Rather than jump straight into business as usual he wanted to experiment with a 'check-in' in order to give people an opportunity to settle into the meeting and more broadly foster relationships, connection and overall communication levels. The 'check-in' questions he asked each individual to respond to changed over time, but were based on asking things such as 'How are you feeling at the moment?', 'What has your attention and focus?', 'What are you grateful for?' or 'What kind of day have you had so far?' The manager said that the first time he did this his team looked at him as if had been replaced by a deranged and demonic doppelganger. People were not used to sharing these kinds of thoughts and reflections openly in what had previously been highly structured and focused meetings. But he persisted. For the first month he said that the 'check-in' felt a bit staged or forced, but after a couple of months these feelings dissipated and it began to feel like standard practice. Over time, as people became more familiar with the concept, they began to open up more, appreciate the voice that it gave everyone and the mutual feelings for trust and connecting it promoted.

As well as requiring vulnerability, making change needs a combination of focus, effort and energy. Unfortunately, these are our most precious and limited commodities during a working day. A 2019 study which investigated energy levels and job crafting found that there was an initial trade-off involved in the short-term efforts of job crafting and the longer-term benefits. As the researchers Arnold Bakker and Wido Oerlemans noted:[4]

> It may take time in order for job crafting to have a favourable impact on work engagement and performance, because the sheer act of job crafting is effortful and can initially be experienced as an additional job demand.

So job crafting, as with any and all change, can deplete energy levels, especially in the short term. Recognizing this is important for people to structure their job crafting efforts in ways that make them compelling to work towards and easiest to complete.

Seven factors for compelling goal setting

Fortunately, research from the fields of goal setting and behaviour change is well developed and there are a number of ideas and strategies that can be deployed to maximize the likelihood of making job crafting goals stick. There are seven factors that are particularly helpful in goal setting.

1. BE COMPELLING AND CLEAR

The first step of the process is choosing the right kind of goal. Having understood the different types of and opportunities for job crafting, people often have a number of ideas that they want to explore to make their work more personal and engaging. Trying to identify and shake out one idea from the number that are available can be hard. I tend to encourage people to go with the idea that best balances personal excitement and curiosity with potential impact, practicality and achievability.

The goals that people set themselves should be crystal clear. There should be no doubt or ambiguity about whether or not you have achieved a goal. One way to increase the clarity of a goal is to apply a 'bright line' rule. From a legal perspective, bright-line rules refer to clearly defined laws or standards that are easy to interpret and clear to spot when they have been transgressed.[5] From a goal-setting perspective, bright lines are rules that will be applied and followed in respect of specific targets and ambitions. So, for example, rather than setting a general relationship job crafting goal of 'giving more thanks to others', a clearer goal, with bright lines, would be, 'every day before turning off my computer I will have sent a note of thanks to a colleague'. Setting and framing the goal in this way makes it easy to understand whether or not you have achieved your target; if you have switched off your computer without having sent a note of thanks that day you have failed to meet your goal. By contrast, if you power down your PC having expressed gratitude to a colleague then you can go home with a smile on your face knowing you've met your goal.

2. START SMALL

There's an avalanche of research from the fields of behavioural economics, psychology and motivation,[6] supported by findings and work from consultants and practitioners, which shows the power and ultimate benefit of breaking larger targets into tiny or micro goals. There are a number of reasons that setting small goals can be effective and set people on a path to potentially larger, more significant change.

First, people approach micro goals with a mindset of curiosity and fun rather than burden and despair. The risks of not achieving the goal are small and consequently people tend to be more experimental in their approach.

A second advantage of setting tiny goals is that most people can find the time to do them. I recommend people set goals that will take five minutes or less, which is less time than it takes to go to the toilet or brew a cup of tea, things that all of us find time for during the day.

Third, setting a micro goal stops people having 'goal creep' and becoming overambitious. Humans are, unfortunately, not good predictors of our abilities to achieve the goals we set ourselves and away from the demands and competing pressures that are waiting for us at our work desk we set unrealistic goals for ourselves in workshops and training sessions. Our future intentions often don't match with our actual behaviours at that time. Whilst running home three times a week rather than driving seems incredibly achievable when sitting in the comfort of a warm meeting room, the reality of doing this at the end of the day when you are feeling mentally and physically exhausted is another thing altogether.

Fourth, a further reason to start small relates to the perceptions and support of others. I find that managers and leaders are more likely to get on board with the idea of job crafting and test the idea if the changes that their team members are going to experiment with are small. Focusing on small crafting changes can temper concerns that people are going to change their jobs in unrealistic and unachievable ways.

Finally, finding small changes means that job crafting is assessable and achievable to a wider variety of jobs. On the surface, people working in call centres or on customer service desks might not appear to have the freedom or the capacity to shape their roles. But when you are only looking to make small changes, the opportunities to craft become more achievable. Funnily enough, I find it is people working in these ostensibly fixed or regulated jobs who get most creative with their job crafting ideas, in part because they are the individuals who crave autonomy the most.

THE POWER OF TINY HABITS

Dr B J Fogg, the Director of the Behaviour Design Lab at Stanford University, is a strong proponent of starting small to encourage and enable behaviour change. Dr Fogg is a psychologist and researcher who has investigated behaviour for over 20 years. He believes that the secret to bigger and bolder goals is to start small. Tiny, in fact. Through his Tiny Habits programme,[7] he encourages people to find, and make the commitment to, the tiniest aspect of a potentially larger goal. For example, he advises people who want to start flossing more regularly to start with a commitment to flossing just one tooth each night, or for those who want to increase their strength, to do two push-ups. Rather than committing to writing for 20 minutes in a diary each night, Dr Fogg would advocate that, in order to embed the habit and routine, it might be more effective to start with writing for a maximum of one minute. The focus on starting small is to achieve large volumes of success (eg being able to do 50 press-ups) but it starts people on a pathway to making a habit automatic, which they can then incrementally build upon.

3. PLAN

Plans, whilst unglamorous, are both potent and powerful for supporting and enabling behaviour change. Findings from psychology, consistently show that by having a plan, people are much more likely to follow through with their intentions and achieve their goals.[8] Rather than simply asking someone what their goal is, it is more powerful and effective to get someone to set out a roadmap to how they are going to achieve their targets including where, when and how they are going to do it.

A study of almost 300,000 people who took part in the Pennsylvania Democratic Party election in 2008 demonstrated just how powerful prompts to plan could be.[9] Calls were made to three different groups of prospective voters. The first group received a standard call reminding them about the upcoming election and asking them to vote. The second group of potential voters were asked whether they planned to vote. The last group were asked only what time they would vote, but also what they would be doing before they voted and where they would be coming from. Effectively, the last group were asked to make a voting plan – they were making a connection between the action of voting and the movements of their day. Individuals who received the standard call were found to be no more likely to vote than if they had not received the call; it had no influence on their voting behaviour. Asking people whether they intended to vote (the second group) was found to have a very small influence of around 2 per cent. The impact of asking planning-oriented questions was found to be the most effective. This third group were found to be 4.1 per cent more likely to vote. And the impact was found to be more potent and profound in households when there was only one voter. These individuals were 9.1 percentage points more likely to vote as the consequence of a planning-oriented call, potentially because they were the least likely to have existing plans.

4. USE ANCHORS, HABITS AND ROUTINES

People are more likely to adopt new habits and behaviours if they incorporate them into existing routines and behaviours. Doing something completely new involves carving out the time and energy do it, summoning sufficient motivation and, of course, remembering to do it in the first place. Consequently, new and novel goals may not be sustainable in the longer term.

Linking new goals with existing habits and routines reduces the conscious control and effort required. In the workplace, people can try to find ways to integrate job crafting into existing ways of working. For example, someone who has a task-crafting goal of planning their day and identifying the key things they want to achieve before diving into work, could use sitting down at their desk first thing in the morning as the anchor or cue for their goal. Rather than turning the computer on and jumping into their email (does that sound familiar?) they can instead use the cue of sitting down to open their calendar and write down two or three key aspects of work they want to have progressed or achieved by the end of the day. Similarly, someone who wanted to capture the most fulfilling aspects of their work each day could put a diary on the seat of their car as a reminder, or alternatively, use the act of sitting down on the bus as a prompt to reach for a diary or notepad.

5. USE REWARDS

Rewards are a positive and potent way of encouraging and consolidating behaviour change.[10] They can satisfy our cravings and give a natural hit of dopamine, which makes us feel good. These rewards don't have to be new or novel, but could be part of your existing routine. For example, a reward could be making your first cup of coffee for the day, checking social media, taking a break or turning on your computer. I encourage people to experiment with different rewards and see what motivates them. For those interested in their health and wellbeing, resisting the reward being something alcoholic or calorific might be useful, particularly if this is something you want to use as an incentive in the long term.

A twist on the concept of getting a reward after you have done something is temptation bundling. Temptation bundling combines the reward with the goal activity or task being undertaken. For example, researchers tested this idea with people who wanted to commit to regular exercise at the gym. They paired the exercise with doing something that the participants found exciting or stimulating which they would look forward to, such as listening to an audiobook of a thrilling story. Participants who were only able to access or to listen to the story when doing exercise were found to visit the gym 51 per cent more frequently than a control group.[11] Applying this idea to job crafting, people could bundle a new goal activity with a treat or something that they find rewarding. For example, someone who committed to parking their car a mile away from the office to enable them to walk to and from work could pair this goal with listening to a favourite podcast, audiobook or piece of music. If protecting times to connect with colleagues is a goal, then you could temptation bundle this by having lunch out at a local café or preparing your favourite items for lunch.

6. INVOLVE OTHERS

People are more likely to be successful in achieving their aims if they are accountable to other people. Effectively, we are more likely to attain a goal when we are not going for it alone. By involving other people you are letting others help you to be successful. By publicly sharing goals you are creating social expectations, and tapping into our innate drive to want to show our human desire to demonstrate competence and success. Studies on accountability have consistently shown that sharing a goal with someone else significantly increases an individual's chance of success.[12] From a job crafting perspective, I encourage people to buddy up with a colleague to share their goal and to make a commitment plan in respect of how they are going to keep in touch with each other. This could be by email or instant messenger, a quick call once a week or a coffee chat if they work nearby. Not only does this keep people motivated to stick to their goals, but it also creates opportunities for peer coaching and support where partners share tips and ideas about sticking to or, if need be, adapting their targets.

Another way to source the benefits of others is through group power. People tend to work more effectively working towards a goal as a collective rather than working individually. This is one of the reasons that group-based healthy eating or weight-loss programmes are so successful. A randomized control study of a Weight Watchers programme found that people lost almost double the amount of weight compared with individuals who were working alone.[13] As behavioural science specialists Owain Swain and Rory Gallagher[14] report, similar results can be used to good effect in the arena of savings. People who formed saving groups and publicly committed to their goals doubled the amount saved compared to individuals. And this was the case even when individuals were offered inducements to save, such as higher interest rates.[15]

In terms of job crafting specifically, a useful way to harness the power of a group is to hold workshops or meetings. In these sessions, people declare to the group the changes that they will be making to the way they do their jobs. I find this works for three reasons. First, it stokes people's motivations because they are accountable to a number of other people. Second, sharing stories enables people to share ideas and tap into the wisdom, experience and enthusiasm of others. Lastly, knowing other people are also shaping their jobs gives people an incentive and encouragement to follow through with their work personalization plans.

7. HOLD A PRE-MORTEM

In medicine, a post-mortem is used to examine a body to determine the cause of death. In project management and product development, post-mortems and retrospectives are commonly used to review and explore the successes, failures and learnings following the completion of a specific activity. These are fantastic at generating and consolidating learning – but the catch is that these insights come about when the project has been delivered or goals and objectives are being reviewed. However, you don't need to wait until a problem or failure occurs to deal with a potential issue. It is possible to generate insights, and develop strategies for overcoming known barriers, in advance of starting a new endeavour and this is through an approach called pre-mortems. Pre-mortems are used and encouraged by the likes of Atlassian[16] and McKinsey,[17] and have been identified as an effective management strategy by researchers.[18]

A pre-mortem takes place before a project or initiative commences or a goal is set in stone. It encourages and enables people to explore the reasons why they, or their team, might fail to achieve their desired outcomes and objectives and to identify all the things that might get in the way. A pre-mortem requires an individual or team to project into the future, and imagine that their project has failed, or their goal has not been reached, and then to explore and identify all the factors which might have led to this negative outcome. Visualizing and identifying risks before they happen enables teams to steer away from them. The pre-mortem also mitigates our natural human tendency to be overconfident in the success of a new project or goal. It also gives people a voice and opportunity to express concerns or limitations they see.

From a job crafting perspective, I encourage people to explore the reasons why they might fail to achieve their chosen goal. Barriers that people often identify include: overcoming and unpicking 'traditional' expectations from managers and colleagues about how a role might be undertaken; rigid structures and policies; and more personal factors including a lack of time, energy and overall motivation. Where possible, I get people to list how they might tackle or overcome a specific barrier. For example, a barrier might be potential lack of support from a manager. A way to mitigate this may be to present an idea as a short-term experiment, rather than a permanent change, and to be specific about how the crafting idea will be of benefit to the individual, but also potentially to their team.

A job crafting goal template

I have developed a specific goal-setting template for participants to use in my job crafting workshops which builds on the psychological and behavioural research we have explored in this chapter. Specifically, I ask participants to consider six different factors when developing and committing to their job crafting goal:

1 **Goal – my job crafting goal.** With as much clarity and concision as possible write down what the job crafting goal is. The clearer and more precise you can be the better. Make your goal small so that it is something that can be achieved in less than 10 minutes a day or an hour a week in total.

2 **Significance – why is this goal important?** Articulate the reasons for setting the job crafting goal. Answering this question gets people to consider why this change matters to them and taps into internal motivations and values.

3 **Trigger – what are my triggers?** Note down any triggers that are associated with the job crafting goal. These triggers are physical or mental cues that prime people to deploy their new job crafting habit.

4 **Barriers – what are the potential barriers?** This requires people to reflect on the practicalities of the goal they are setting and the different hurdles, headwinds and hindrances which might prevent people from achieving their goal.

5 **Reward – how am I going to reward myself?** Note down how you are going to recognize or celebrate the achievement of the goal. This could be anything. It could be making a cup of coffee, having a break, giving yourself a pat on the back, a break to catch up with social media. Ultimately, participants need to identify a reward that is meaningful to them.

6 **Accountability – who am I going to be accountable to? And how are we going to check in?** I ask participants to identify an accountability buddy who they are going to share their goal with. Asking them to consider how they are going to check in with each other gets people to start to plan and identify opportunities to speak, which makes it more likely to happen.

GOAL-SETTING EXAMPLE 1
Expressing gratitude to others

Sue, a customer services manager, wants to intentionally spend time recognizing the positive aspects of her work. She also wants to ensure that other people know that she values their efforts, talents and skills and more broadly wants to encourage people to get in the habit of giving positive feedback to others. She decides to set herself a job crafting goal of expressing gratitude to others more. Working through the checklist encourages Sue to be more specific about and deliberate about the goal:

Goal? – To express thanks to a colleague by email, phone or in person once a day.

Why? – I value the contribution of others, and recognize we work as a whole team. I also feel good thanking others and like the fact that it makes others feel good too.

Trigger? – I'll set a diary reminder at 16.30 each day to remind me to send a note of thanks. If I haven't found an opportunity to say thank you that day, I'll do it in response to this reminder.

Barrier? – Some days there may not be clear opportunities and things to be grateful for. On these days I will think about some of the wider benefits of my job that I value and appreciate.

Reward? – My reward is the feel-good factor I get from saying thanks to others. I'll also finish my day having recently done something positive, which will put me a good frame of mind to leave work.

Buddy? – My buddy will be my partner at home. I'll tell her about who I thanked that day over dinner together.

GOAL-SETTING EXAMPLE 2
Learning to be more evidence-based

Michael, an HR manager, is curious about how to introduce a more evidence-based decision-making process to the function. His job crafting goal in the first instance is to commit a total of one hour a week to researching and reading about the concept, with the intention to run a session for the HR team about this at a forthcoming awayday. Rather than simply putting an hour into his diary, which he knows will be the first thing he lets go of when pressured for time, he commits to spending 10–15 minutes at the start of each day researching, reading articles and reaching out to contacts through Twitter and LinkedIn.

Goal? – To spend 15 minutes at the start of each day researching and compiling information about evidence-based learning and then reflecting on whether, and how, this could be implemented within our team.

Why? – I'm personally interested in this – I want to develop my knowledge and skills. Additionally, from what I've seen and read to date, I think this approach could be valuable to the team and organization as a whole.

Trigger? – Before opening emails at the start of the day, I will spend 10–15 minutes (which I'll time) researching and reading articles.

Barrier? – Some days, I might forget or be too busy with another urgent task. I'll put a Post-it note next to my computer in an attempt to remind me. On the days where I don't have time, I'll try to schedule the research for another time, or just miss a day and pick up again at the next opportunity.

Reward? – I'm really interested in learning and developing – so my reward will be the knowledge gained and the satisfaction of having done something personally interesting and important before the day starts.

Buddy? – My buddy will be my line manager. I'm going to keep her updated at our one-to-ones.

This goal-setting framework does not have to be a checklist. You don't have to complete every stage, but research and my practical experience suggest that the more of these areas you think about and address, the higher the likelihood that you will be successful in achieving your goal.

Job crafting examples

When sharing the job crafting goal template, people often ask for examples of crafting that others have set themselves. Below are listed a number of examples of different job crafting activities that people could do, and in my experience have done, in less than 10 minutes a day or an hour a week in total. I encourage people to use this list or other examples they see as a stimulus for their own goal, rather than something to copy or select from. The power and purpose of job crafting comes from individuals creating their own goal that resonates and engages with them personally.

MICRO JOB CRAFTING EXAMPLES

Task + skill crafting

- Do something else each day for the benefit of a colleague(s).
- Make suggestions to change a system or process.
- Volunteer for a new project.
- Read an article or research a topic.
- Change locations to complete different aspects of your work.
- Perform a routine task in a different way.

Relationship crafting

- Speak in person to a colleague rather than emailing them.
- Learn something new about a team member.
- Attend or initiate a team activity.
- Have lunch with a work friend.
- Shadow a colleague for an hour.
- Practise active listening to deepen connections with others.

Purpose crafting

- Learn more about the people you are helping/your customers.
- Explore your work's wider organizational purpose.
- Explore your personal values and how these align to the work you do.
- Keep a file note/record of the impact you are having in your role.
- Reflect each day on the person you helped the most.
- Follow up with customers or colleagues you have helped in the past and explore how your work helped them.

Wellbeing crafting

- Hold walking 1:1 meetings.
- Take the stairs each day rather than the lift.
- Bring in healthy office snacks.
- Work in deliberate chunks with intentional breaks.
- Take a full lunch break.
- Park a mile away from work and walk into the office and back to the car once a week.

Making job crafting habits stick

When I discuss goal setting, I often ask people how long they think it takes to form a habit. The most popular response is often silence. And then someone tends to share something they've read or heard that it takes between 21 and 30 days to form a habit. This is an idea that appears to have been popularized in our day-to-day media, like the need to take 10,000 steps a day for health,[19] that has no empirical support behind it. It's bad science. Counter to popular belief, there is no specific number of days, or magic number of repetitions that result in habit formation. Unhelpful, I know. The time taken to form habits is influenced by a number of factors, including motivation, magnitude of the new behaviour and social support from others. Research published in the *European Journal of Social Psychology* by Dr Phillippa Lally and her colleagues[20] set out to investigate how long it takes to form a new habit or routine. Over a 12-week period they followed 96 participants who were trying to introduce new behaviours and routines into their lives which ranged from drinking a bottle of water over lunch, to running 15 minutes per day before dinner. The researchers found that it took on average more than two months – 66 days to be precise – for participants to report new behaviours becoming automatic and routine.

The reality is that job crafting changes won't become habit overnight. They need constant reinforcement and practice. It will likely take weeks and possibly months for new ways of working, and thinking about work, to become routine. To provide support and encouragement along this journey I suggest people who have made job crafting goals in groups and teams come together. Sharing experiences and getting encouragement from others can provide motivation to enable people to tweak or stick to their plans to personalize their work.

Conclusion

Job crafting involves a two-step process – identifying a change that you want to make, and then physically doing it. Neither of these two steps are always straightforward and easy, but fortunately there are a number of known steps, tricks and hacks that we can use to increase the likelihood of our success. Exploring critical questions around different themes such as who?, why?, what?, when?, where?, and well? can encourage us to identify different elements of our jobs that we would like to craft and customize. Setting small and clear crafting targets and goals with rigour and clarity increases the likelihood of success, as does involving others, and having clear rewards.

In addition to holding workshops and setting job crafting goals, there are a number of other ways that organizations can intentionally support and enable people to specifically job craft or more broadly tailor and shape their work. We will explore these in the next chapter and outline ways in which organizations can encourage job crafting as a mindset where improving and innovating how work is done is a constant and consistent endeavour.

KEY POINTS

- Critical, coaching-focused questions can encourage people to reflect on how they currently approach and value work and can stimulate ideas and opportunities to job craft.

- Six themes of questions which stimulate reflection are why?, well?, what?, who?, when?, where?

- People can influence the success of their job crafting attempts by being clear on the goal they are striving for and starting small in terms of the size of the change they are making.

- Setting effective job crafting goals involves six components: establishing a clear goal, exploring why it is significant, identifying a trigger, exploring barriers, being clear on rewards, and sourcing social support.

- It takes time and energy for job crafting to become a habit.

- The time it takes job crafting to become a habit is influenced by factors such as size of the change, individual motivation and organizational support.

KEY QUESTIONS

- How regularly do people have an opportunity to consider some, or any, of the question themes outlined in the chapter?

- Are there any specific questions that are relevant to you personally, or to people within your organization?

- What is the organizational approach to goal setting? How effective are people at setting and achieving meaningful goals?

Notes

1   Newport, C (2016) *Deep Work: Rules for focused success in a distracted world*, Hachette UK

2   Newport, C (2016) On using inspiring locations to inspire deeper work, available at: http://www.calnewport.com/blog/2016/04/01/on-using-inspiring-locations-to-inspire-deeper-work/ (archived at https://perma.cc/9RNE-H9UQ)

3   Norcross, J C, Ratzin, A C and Payne, D (1989) Ringing in the New Year: the change processes and reported outcomes of resolutions, *Addictive Behaviors*, **14** (2), pp 205–12

4   Bakker, A B and Oerlemans, W G (2019) Daily job crafting and momentary work engagement: a self-determination and self-regulation perspective, *Journal of Vocational Behavior*, **112**, pp 417–30

5   Gillespie, D T (1999) Bright-line rules: development of the law of search and seizure during traffic stops. *Loyola University Chicago Law Journal*, **31**, p.1

6   Service, O and Gallagher, R (2017) *Think Small: The surprisingly simple ways to reach big goals*, Michael O'Mara Books

7   Fogg, B J (nd) Tiny Habits, available at: https://www.tinyhabits.com/ (archived at https://perma.cc/6WGL-8K45)

8   Service, O and Gallagher, R (2017) (see note 6 above)

9   Nickerson, D W and Rogers, T (2010) Do you have a voting plan? Implementation intentions, voter turnout, and organic plan making, *Psychological Science*, **21** (2), pp 194–99

10 Duhigg, C (2013) *The Power of Habit: Why we do what we do and how to change*, Random House

11 Milkman, K L, Minson, J A and Volpp, K G (2013) Holding the Hunger Games hostage at the gym: an evaluation of temptation bundling, *Management Science*, **60** (2), pp 283–99

12 Service, O and Gallagher, R (2017) (see note 6 above)

13 Jebb, S A *et al* (2011) Primary care referral to a commercial provider for weight loss treatment versus standard care: a randomised controlled trial, *The Lancet*, **378** (9801), pp 1485–92

14 Service, O and Gallagher, R (2017) (see note 6 above)

15 Kast, F, Meier, S and Pomeranz, D (2012) Under-savers anonymous: evidence on self-help groups and peer pressure as a savings commitment device (No. w18417), National Bureau of Economic Research

16 Premortem, definition, available at: https://www.atlassian.com/team-playbook/plays/pre-mortem (archived at https://perma.cc/JF4Y-WA7Z)

17 Klein, G, Koller, T and Lovallo, D (2019) Bias busters: premortems: being smart at the start, *McKinsey*, available at: https://www.mckinsey.com/business-functions/strategy-and-corporate-finance/our-insights/bias-busters-premortems-being-smart-at-the-start (archived at https://perma.cc/QLT5-XHK9)

18 Owen, C (2017) Leadership, communication and teamwork in emergency management, in *Human Factors Challenges in Emergency Management* (pp. 125–48), CRC Press

19 Cox, D (2018) Watch your step: why the 10,000 daily goal is built on bad science, *Guardian*, available at: https://www.theguardian.com/lifeandstyle/2018/sep/03/watch-your-step-why-the-10000-daily-goal-is-built-on-bad-science (archived at https://perma.cc/J9FS-Z7NE)

20 Lally, P *et al* (2010) How are habits formed: modelling habit formation in the real world, *European Journal of Social Psychology*, **40** (6), 998–1009

PART THREE

Encourage

07

Exercises and activities to encourage job crafting

Encouraging job crafting

The tricky thing about job crafting is that you can't force it. By its very nature, job crafting is something that has to be proactively driven by an individual or team. For gardeners, it's a similar problem with planting seeds. You can't force a seed to germinate. Fortunately, whilst you can't control it, there is a wealth of knowledge and guidance available to gardeners to determine which combination of temperature, soil and light maximizes the chances for growth. Similarly, with job crafting, there are a number of exercises, tools and activities which have been developed to help bring the concept to life for individuals, teams and organizations.

This chapter will provide an overview of seven different exercises which support and encourage job crafting discussions and create opportunities for people to tailor, shape and personalize their approach to work. The exercises and tools are summarized in Table 7.1 and explored individually below.

Job crafting exercises and workshops

The most direct way to encourage job crafting is to hold sessions and activities with this specific objective. Simplistically, this involves creating the space and opportunity for people to explore how they do their job – where they are spending their time and energy, where they find meaning, what tasks and activities they complete and the interactions they have with others. Job crafting workshops provide people with the knowledge and tools to

TABLE 7.1   Exercises and activities which support job crafting

Exercise	Focus	Format
Job crafting exercises and workshops	Introducing job crafting and opportunities for people to find ways to craft their jobs and set job crafting goals.	Small group/team; 1:1 with line manager or coach; individually.
Energy mapping	Exploring the different aspects of work that people find energizing and draining and how much time they spend on these activities.	Small group/team; 1:1 with line manager or coach; individually.
Job canvas	Uncovering the core value of work and mapping out the different dimensions and elements of a job.	Small group/team; 1:1 with line manager or coach; individually.
Best future work self	Exploring an employee's best future work self and using this as a stimulus to identify opportunities for growth and development.	Small group/team; 1:1 with line manager or coach; individually.
Crafting conversations	Active one-to-one conversations which explore how to personalize and make work better.	1:1 with line manager or coach.
Exploring and applying strengths	Uncovering and exploring individual strengths and how to apply and amplify them at work.	Small group/team; 1:1 with line manager or coach; individually.
Team crafting	Creating opportunities for team members to collaboratively and collectively job craft and swap, dial up and dial down different elements of their jobs.	Small group/team.

explore personal values, passions and strengths and reflect on how they can amplify and bring these to work.

CONTENT AND STRUCTURE OF WORKSHOPS

At the 2019 World Positive Psychology Congress in Melbourne, Australia, I was invited to speak and share my experiences of designing and delivering job crafting workshops. I co-delivered this session with Dr Machteld

TABLE 7.2   An overview of a 'standard' two-hour job crafting introductory workshop

Section	Content
What is job crafting?	• Different types of job crafting • Different sizes of job crafting • Examples of job crafting (context specific to the organization)
Why job craft? The needs and the evidence	• The benefits of job crafting for organizations • The benefits of job crafting for leaders • The benefits of job crafting for individuals
Group exploration	• Have participants job crafted before? • What do they see as the benefits of job crafting? • What do they see as the drawbacks of job crafting? • What are the organizational barriers? How can they be overcome?
How to craft	• Different strategies to encourage job crafting • Ideas for job crafting
Setting a (small) job crafting goal	• Setting a small job crafting goal • Sharing and discussing goal with other participants

(Maggie) Van den Heuvel, who was the lead author on the first ever published job crafting intervention study.[1] Dr Van den Heuvel is not only a leading scholar of job crafting, she also consults with and supports organizations to introduce, encourage and evaluate job crafting workshops. Whilst Maggie and I work in different countries with different audiences, when we discussed our approach we found that the core framework and content of our workshops was similar. Table 7.2 gives a high-level overview of the content of our sessions which we shared at the 2019 World Congress.

The workshops I run are designed to give people the confidence, encouragement and excitement to actively experiment with, and explore, job crafting. My test for whether people fully understand the concept of job crafting is whether they feel confident and able to explain the idea to a friend or colleague. In terms of exploring the concept, I ask people to share examples of where they might have job crafted previously (often without realizing this was what they were doing). When inviting people to set a job crafting goal, I generally challenge them to make a small change which takes less than 10 minutes a day or an hour a week (we explored the reason for this in Chapter 6).

To evaluate the success of the workshops, I ask people to take a job craft-ing questionnaire. I typically resend the questionnaire again one, three and twelve months later, often as part of follow-up workshops to capture and understand whether and how people are using job crafting in their work.

Through the data we collect as a company we've found that to date 86 per cent of people who have learnt about job crafting in Tailored Thinking workshops have actively applied and experimented with the concept in their work, which is higher than the typical learning transfers rates from training sessions, estimated at 30–60 per cent.[2] Anecdotally, other job craft-ing coaches and trainers report similar results. In part, I think the explanation for this is that people are curious about how they can make their work better and create a better fit between their work and themselves as individuals.

OTHER JOB CRAFTING INTERVENTIONS

In addition to the general approach that I outline there are a number of other ways to approach and encourage job crafting in structured and infor-mal ways.

One specific intervention to note is the Job Crafting Exercise[TM 3] which was developed in 2008 by Assistant Professor Justin Berg, Professor Jane Dutton and Professor Amy Wrzesniewski. The last two names in this list might sound familiar as they are the academics who were the first to describe and define job crafting in their 2001 research paper. The specific Job Crafting Exercise[TM] and iterations of it have been used in a number of job crafting intervention studies.[4]

The Job Crafting Exercise[TM] is a visual and interactive activity involving a number of stages. Firstly, individuals complete a 'before sketch' of their work with the purpose of understanding how they currently spend their time and energy across the series of tasks that comprise their job. Secondly, the exer-cise involves allocating the individual tasks into one of three different 'task blocks' according to where people spend the most time and energy. Thirdly, participants create an 'after sketch', which involves sketching out what an ideal role would look like for them. Lastly, the exercise involves creating a job crafting action plan involving clear short- and long-term goals.

ENCOURAGING PARTICIPATION

My personal view would be that attendance at job crafting training sessions should be encouraged but never forced. By definition, job crafting is something that is proactive and has to be driven by the individuals themselves. It is not something therefore that can be mandated. Similarly, a job crafting goal can't be created by a colleague or line manager and 'given' to an individual – the essence of job crafting is that it is employee-driven and therefore goals need to be created, crafted and shaped individually by the employee.

If people are not interested or able to attend a job crafting training session – or any training session for that matter – I hope that leaders are at least curious about why this is the case. It could be that people already feel confident and able to shape their work, or really happy with how their jobs are currently structured. Or they simply don't think the concept or session would benefit them professionally. These are sound and clear explanations. But there could be other less visible reasons for not attending training which are useful to consider and rule out. These could include managers who fear job crafting, explicitly or subtly discouraging colleagues from attending sessions, or employees simply not having the time, energy and motivation to attend. People experiencing work overload are not always easy to spot, yet these are the very individuals who could find elements of job crafting particularly valuable. Wherever possible these potential barriers or hurdles should be identified and tackled in the most appropriate way – such as (further) education for managers, and positive steps to address workload challenges.

Energy mapping

People naturally have a sense of the activities and tasks at work that light them up and those that drain energy away from them. An exercise I use with individuals, which can be adapted for teams, is to list 10–15 key activities that are core and important parts of their current roles and to reflect how much energy they give or take away. I recommend participants use a generic scale from –10 to +10 for this. Having mapped energy levels, I ask people to reflect on how much time they spend on the different tasks. If people have access to sticky notes and a white board, or masking tape and a wall, they can plot their energy and time investment and expenditure on a graph (see Figure 7.1). This mapping exercise allows people to reflect on, and see the interplay between, the time they spend on tasks and their energy load.

If people are able to plot their results on a graph I encourage them to focus on two areas in particular. The first area is at the far top left (high-lighted in Figure 7.1). This area reflects activities where people are spending

FIGURE 7.1   Time and Energy Task Map

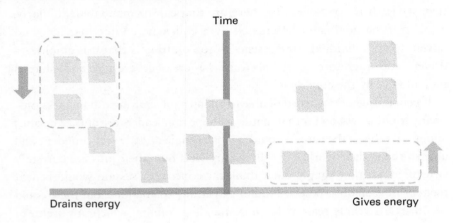

a lot of time but which are draining or taking away energy. These tasks could have a significant impact on people's overall enjoyment of and engagement with their job. I suggest that people reflect on what it is about these tasks that they find so draining and whether there are opportunities to shape or change aspects of the task. For example, they might be able to make changes to the physical requirements of the activities (task crafting), learn new ways to perform the task (skill crafting) or explore the purpose and value of the task (purpose crafting).

The second area of the Time and Energy Task Map that warrants specific consideration is the area on the bottom-right-hand side of the graph. These tasks represent potential hidden gems. These are activities that people don't spend much time on, but when they do, they find that they give them energy and often enjoyment. I encourage people to explore what it is about these activities that gives them energy and to consider whether there are any ways in which they can do more of, or amplify and build upon, these activities in their work.

Through discussion and reflection this exercise allows an individual to consider their current allocation of personal resources of time and energy and what opportunities there are to shape and change these to maximize their energy, and meet their needs for control, positive self-identity and connection with others.

ENERGY MAPPING CASE STUDY
A newsletter that takes time and drains energy

Bethanie, an Internal Communications Lead, undertook the energy mapping exercise. She noted that she found the task of compiling content for the company's monthly internal newsletter a big time commitment, but also a drain and something that she came to dread. She described how sourcing news items and stories was often a challenge. More broadly, she was becoming increasingly unsure of the value and relevance of the newsletter itself, particularly in terms of who was reading it and what people took interest in. Her feelings about the newsletter had changed over time – when she first joined the company she really enjoyed pulling together stories and news items, in part because she was still learning about the company herself.

Through asking a number of questions about how the tasks could be done differently (based on the questions outlined in Chapter 6) she identified a number of ways in which she could redesign or re-energize the activity of compiling the newsletter to make it more meaningful and stimulating. Some of the ideas Bethanie had were:

- holding a focus group about the newsletter to understand its value (purpose and relationship crafting);

- developing a questionnaire to capture views about the newsletter (purpose crafting);

- learning how to use the analytics aspect of the content management system to view click-through rates on different articles to understand what areas were of most interest to colleagues and whether there were standing items or information that people weren't engaging with (skill crafting, purpose crafting);

- looking for new content and ideas for the newsletter, including interviewing a different employee each month (relationship crafting, task crafting);

- redesigning the layout and design of the newsletter (task crafting, skill crafting);

- involving other people from across the organization in compiling the newsletter and creating content (relationship crafting, task crafting);

- exploring new and different alternatives to a company newsletter which still allowed information to be shared and encouraged communication more broadly (skill crafting, task crafting).

At the end of five minutes of brainstorming, Bethanie was visibly excited about how to refresh the newsletter. The exercise had made her realize that whilst she hadn't lost interest in the importance of communicating with and engaging people from across the organization, she had become bored with how she was performing this task.

ENERGY MAPPING CASE STUDY (CONTINUED)
Training delivery

Ben, an HR officer, used the energy mapping exercise to identify and tap into an area of HR work that he enjoyed but had not previously found a way to incorporate into his current role.

Through the exercise, Ben identified that one of the things he loved doing in his role was training delivery. This was not a specific requirement of his job and was something he spent little time doing. But a few recent experiences of supporting training sessions had shown him that this was both something he really liked and something that he was good at. In particular, he had enjoyed thinking about training design and having the opportunity to bring people together from different parts of the business area he supported. Through reflection and discussions with others, Ben identified a number of ways that he could subtly shape his role to build upon his existing experience, and create new opportunities to deliver training. These included:

- volunteering to support the company's learning and development team on the delivery of relevant HR training courses where he could provide some input and expertise (task crafting, relationship crafting);
- undertaking some self-study about facilitation skills and the design of training and development approaches and strategies (skill crafting);
- developing training sessions to deliver to the business areas he supported to help them deal with specific issues that they were facing – for example, refreshers on how to hold performance discussions, managing performance etc (task crafting);
- holding monthly HR drop-in sessions, which would bring managers together from across the business (task crafting, relationship crafting).

Using a job canvas

Once developed, traditional job descriptions are seldom regularly referred to. At best a job specification is used for advertising new positions and then dusted down and brought out before performance discussions or promotion reviews. An alternative way of presenting and representing a job is through a job canvas.

The job canvas is a dynamic document which encourages people to consider the core value of the role and identify the people and processes they influence and those that influence them. The job canvas (shown in Figure 7.2) was initially developed to define individual roles, but it has also been used by functional and project teams to capture and outline the scope of their work. Typically, it takes 15–20 minutes to develop a sketch outline of each job and 20–40 minutes to complete a detailed job overview.

This canvas uses the structure of the business model canvas initially developed by Alexander Osterwalder,[5] but section titles have been changed. Further details about the business and original canvas can be found at Strategyzer.com.

I developed the job canvas with two key aims. First, it is a document that can be quickly and easily changed and updated allowing people to keep 'live' records of the jobs they do, which is helpful in sustaining work focus and purpose and 1:1 and team discussions about work direction. Second, the job canvas encourages people to get to the core, or DNA if you like, of a job or role. The canvas encourages people to move beyond thinking about their job as a set of tasks and activities and can unlock job crafting opportunities for individuals and teams, creating new ways to shape or change aspects of work.

Fascinatingly (for me at least), two people doing ostensibly the same role may produce two different job canvases. For example, one HR business partner might see the senior leader in the function they support as their key and primary customer, whereas others might feel that all people within their function areas are equally significant. Similarly, as we saw in Chapter 3, Amy Wrzesniewski and Jane Dutton found that hospital cleaners would describe the value and significance of their work very differently despite doing the same role. If these employees were asked to complete a job canvas you would expect variations under the columns of Value, Key customers and Key deliverables. Importantly, there is no right or wrong answer in how the canvas is completed. But the way people complete the canvas may be enlightening for managers and colleagues about how an individual might see or perceive their role. For instance, a manager may wonder why a colleague spends a disproportionate amount of time supporting certain customers compared with others – and it might simply be that they see them as more important or significant. Completing the job canvas would shine a light on this.

Exploring a best future work self

A powerful way to lift people's thinking about work is to get them to peer into the future. Specifically, research has shown that asking employees to

FIGURE 7.2 The job canvas

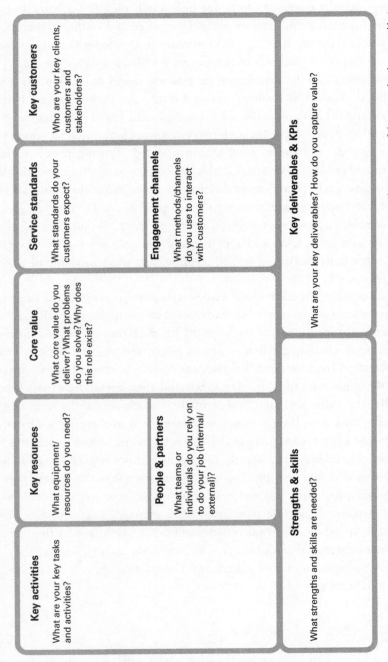

Key activities

What are your key tasks and activities?

Key resources

What equipment/resources do you need?

People & partners

What teams or individuals do you rely on to do your job (internal/external)?

Core value

What core value do you deliver? What problems do you solve? Why does this role exist?

Service standards

What standards do your customers expect?

Engagement channels

What methods/channels do you use to interact with customers?

Key customers

Who are your key clients, customers and stakeholders?

Strengths & skills

What strengths and skills are needed?

Key deliverables & KPIs

What are your key deliverables? How do you capture value?

SOURCE The Job Canvas is a derivative of the Business Model Canvas which can be found at Strategyzer.com. The structure of the canvas has been used but themes have been changed. It is licensed under a Creative Commons Attribution-NonCommercial-NoDerivatives 4.0 International Licence.

explore a positive future work self tends to lift their perspectives, making them more open and alert to opportunities for progression and growth, and more proactive in career planning and development.[6] A future work self is an individual's representation of herself or himself in the future which reflects her or his hopes and aspirations for their work.[7]

With colleagues, Professor Sharon Parker, Director of the Centre for Transformative Work Design at Curtin University (whose work we explored earlier), has studied the significance and influence that having a clear future work self can have. And it turns out that the more developed and defined the image of the future self the better. As she explained to me, 'People with clearer, more assessable and salient visions of their future tend to adopt more proactive career behaviour, such as setting goals, developing skills and abilities and pursuing new experiences.' Professor Parker believes that part of the reason for this link is that a salient image of a future work self can be a tremendous motivational resource.

Having a clear image of a future work self enables and encourages people to do things in their work that they might not otherwise have had the courage or conviction to try. Professor Parker explains that without understanding how it might benefit them in the future, people may be reluctant to proactively change things about their jobs, particularly if they feel it is going to be difficult or challenging. For an example close to home, Professor Parker highlights the challenges faced by some of her PhD students: 'For those that are introverted, the idea of networking and presenting at conferences is a terrifying prospect. They would rather stay in their hotel room than actively create opportunities to build connections with other researchers at conferences.' These fears can be overcome, or tempered, by enabling students to explore and create a clear and salient sense of their future self. Those students who see themselves as an established academic and researcher quickly recognize that their future career will involve a rich variety of connections and collaborative partnerships. Professor Parker goes on to say, 'Knowing that these relationships will be part of a positive future can be a stimulus for the students to more proactively seek opportunities to meet others. They know that, for example, networking at a conference or presenting a paper is a natural first step towards where and who they want to be from a career perspective.' A more future-focused approach to development conversations can also create a strong stimulus for people to personalize their work and job craft. As she explains, 'When you're asking people about their careers you are effectively asking them to think about their future work self; by creating a clear picture of what this looks like you are creating the stimulus and opportunity for people to think, "Okay, well how am I going to craft my job to get me to my future work self?"'

Of course, not everyone will be able to achieve their dream job or role. A number of different external and internal factors might mean that people are not able, or may not even want to be appointed into the positions coveted by their younger selves. For this reason, Professor Parker recommends that where possible people develop a richer 'multidimensional' view of the future which recognizes a number of different career tracks and job opportunities. As she told me, if people are too specific about their future goals this could close an individual's mind off to other opportunities and heighten the risk of negative feelings such as failure if their highly specific future doesn't materialize.

For leaders and line managers, a key take-away is that employees may benefit more by shifting the focus of career conversations away from the current time and immediate future and focusing more on exploring longer-term aspirations and developing a vision for what a future work self might look like. Exercises and activities to do this include drawing mental and physical pictures of your future work self and exploring what 'a day in your future life' would entail. These playful approaches have been found to be particularly effective in engaging people and broadening their perspectives.[8]

Crafting conversations

Managers and team leaders can give encouragement and create the space for people to reflect on how to make their jobs better. Through informal check-ins, traditional 'one to ones' or development-focused sessions, managers can encourage colleagues to reflect on the areas of their job that they could change or tailor to create a better personal fit with their individual passions, talents and strengths.

Managers and line managers can hold discussions with colleagues about their ideas to make their work better and actively encourage them to make changes to see if they have a positive and beneficial impact on them and others. Chapter 6 provides a number of questions that could fuel and facilitate discussions and opposite are some questions that team leaders could ask to help develop ideas for job crafting.

Task crafting

- How could your job be made better? What would you need to do? What, if any, support do you need?

- In an ideal world, what aspects of your job would you do more of? What would you do less of? Why?

Skill crafting

- What skills or knowledge are you most interested in developing further? Why is this?

- In 10 years' time what would be your dream job, internal or external to the organization? What skills and experiences do you need to develop further to achieve this?

Relationship crafting

- What are your strongest relationships at work (in your team, the wider organization, external to the organization)?

- What relationships would you like to build further?

Purpose crafting

- What gives you the greatest sense of accomplishment in your work? Why do you think this is?

- Who do you feel benefits most from the work you do (internal and/or external to the organization)?

Wellbeing crafting

- What changes could be made to your job to improve your health and wellbeing?

- How could you bring more activity into your job?

We will see in Chapter 8 a case study involving Connect Health demonstrating how these coaching conversations can be embedded into development and performance conversations.

Exploring and applying strengths

From a job crafting perspective, knowing personal strengths can be really useful. If you craft your work in ways that build on and amplify strengths, not only are you more likely to find your experiences enjoyable, but they will ultimately be more successful and sustainable too. Focusing on strengths is not something that comes naturally to most people; instead we find it easier to identify foibles and failures.

Human brains are typically wired with a deficit perspective or negativity bias.[9] This often leads us to have a tendency to focus on the problems rather than positives of our work and explains our urge to fixate on the aspects of our jobs and personal lives that we feel aren't working. Psychologists and neuroscientists don't know why this is, but one of the most compelling explanations is that this deficit perspective has been developed to help and ensure our survival as a species. From a survival perspective, it serves us better to be alert to dangers than to focus on and look out for positive experiences. The unfortunate consequence of this evolutionary quirk is that whilst it makes us good at spotting and focusing on failure, it doesn't naturally encourage or enable us to understand or explore our personal strengths or factors that lead to success. This is problematic, as it is building on our strengths rather than fixing our weaknesses that often enables us to do our best work.

The ability to perform optimally, either as a collective or as an individual, tends to come when we are building on and tapping into our strengths. Our strengths can be simply defined as the things we are good at and enjoy doing. A study of over 5,000 people from New Zealand[10] found that people who reported knowing their strengths were nine times more likely to flourish psychologically than those who didn't. And those that knew and used their strengths were 19 times more likely to be thriving at work compared with those who didn't. These results remained consistent irrespective of gender, ethnicity, age, education and income.

The Corporate Leadership Council found similar results when it conducted a study of over 19,000 employees across 29 countries and 34 companies.[11] Highlighting performance strengths as part of check-ins and performance discussions was linked to an increase in overall individual performance of over 36 per cent. By contrast, focusing on performance weakness was linked to negative impact, or cost, of 26 per cent.

One approach researchers recommend to capture individual strengths is to note down experiences during the working week where you felt a blend of energy, focus, engagement and expertise.[12] When searching for strengths people can look for three attributes: firstly, things they are good at and enjoy doing; secondly, patterns of thinking, feeling or behaving that, when exercised, excite, engage and energize; and thirdly, the things that allow people to perform at their best with skill and confidence.

An alternative way to identify strengths is to take a strength-based assessment. These are available online and can be done individually or with a coach. There are a number of tools available, and Dr Michelle McQuaid's book *Your Strengths Blueprint* provides a useful summary of the empirical and practical strengths and limitations of some of the more popular tools available.[13]

Building on the research highlighting the potency of strengths, I encourage people in job crafting workshops to actively explore their personal strengths and the extent to which they are used in their day-to-day work. Job crafting provides an opportunity for people to explore how they can use more of their strengths in their work. For example, an HR manager with a strength related to curiosity or a love of learning could set a skill-crafting goal of researching topics of interest such as positive psychology and exploring how they could bring this to the workplace.

Strengths can also be really useful in achieving the goals and targets we set ourselves. For example, if someone has a strength related to building connections with others, they could draw on this by actively sharing their job crafting goals with colleagues and friends and use the discussion of how they are getting on as an opportunity to catch up.

Team crafting

Rather than being a purely individual pursuit, job crafting can be done collaboratively in teams and team crafting has been found to have a range of benefits.[14,15] A way to encourage team crafting is to facilitate open conversations amongst team members about the different aspects of their work, and in particular the parts they enjoy and find rewarding and the elements they dislike or find a chore. Through positive discussions and collaborative negotiation team members may be able to swap different tasks amongst themselves or change how they collectively tackle certain activities. It allows individuals to dial down on specific tasks or activities in order to create opportunities to cultivate or invest time and energy in others. Teams at Google have successfully used team and collaborative job crafting and job swaps to better align the allocation of work amongst their teams to reflect individual strengths, passions and interests. These have yielded positive results for both individuals and the organization.[16]

Personally, I would have really valued the opportunity to team craft with colleagues when I was an HR generalist. I have always found employee relations work an element of HR work that was less rewarding and engaging than other elements. By comparison, there were colleagues I worked with who loved supporting managers through investigations and chairing disciplinary and grievance hearings. A team-crafting session would have given me the opportunity to share with colleagues that given the choice I would do less employee relations work and ideally more policy and strategy development. Similarly, colleagues who enjoyed case work more than strategy work could have swapped these elements with me. This is not to say that I would have stopped doing case work altogether – as a generalist it is important to maintain and develop experience in this area – but rather than doing it on a routine basis, I could have contributed to the team when there was a high case load or a particularly tricky matter which I was best placed to lead on.

Implementation considerations

Before any intervention, workshop or training initiative is selected there are a number of factors to be considered which have the potential to influence the impact and outcomes:

1 **Facilitators.** The impact of the exercises described in this chapter will be shaped considerably by the expertise, interest and encouragement of the people leading them. For example, job crafting workshops are brought to life by facilitators who are passionate and knowledgeable about the subject and able to give practical examples of how other people have crafted their roles.

2 **Context.** Understanding context is critical in determining which, if any, of the exercises described in the chapter to explore. For example, team crafting is less likely to be effective if a spirit of openness and collaboration does not exist within colleagues and similarly the impact of job crafting workshops is likely to be diminished if there is no capacity or space for people to genuinely explore the ideas and experiment with their jobs after the workshops.

3 **Evidence base.** Before implementing or experimenting with any exercise or activity, it's important to understand what you are trying to change and have confidence that there's evidence that the idea you are testing has the potential to deliver this. For example, research[17] suggests that job crafting workshops are most effective when participants have the support

of their line managers to craft. If it is known that there will no or limited support for people to do this experimentation, then the evidence would suggest that this would not be an effective intervention.

4 **Engagement and interest.** It's important to recognize that not everyone will engage with, and be excited by, the idea of job crafting or discovering and using their strengths. For some people, for a variety of different reasons, they may not want to or feel able to explore these ideas. As job crafting is employee-led and driven, it is not possible – or even desirable – to force someone to proactively shape their role. For these reasons, as explored earlier in this chapter, I always recommend that job crafting sessions are voluntary.

Some evidence-based job crafting questions

Before working with any organization to explore job crafting, or any other kind of initiative, I encourage them to consider whether or not they are clear on why they want to do this and that they have gathered, and have confidence in, the necessary evidence. Whilst it might seem counterintuitive for a consultant to challenge a client's thinking and potentially a commission, ultimately the organization and my consultancy will benefit from having positive and impactful results.

Adapted and informed by the work of Rob Briner and Neil Walshe[18] on developing an evidence-based approach to workplace wellbeing interventions, some questions an organization might want to consider before implementing any form of job crafting initiative include:

- What is the problem we are trying to solve?
- What is the evidence that an intervention such as job crafting is needed?
- What would happen if we didn't do anything?
- What is known about the causes of the problem within the organization?
- Why are we going to encourage people to job craft? What is wrong with people's current approach to working?
- What does published evidence suggest is the cause of the problem? What is the quality of the evidence?
- What does published evidence suggest are the potential benefits of introducing job crafting?

- What factors do we expect job crafting to influence? What is the evidence for this?
- Will the benefits of the job crafting intervention outweigh the costs? Are there other approaches to work design that may be equally or more effective than job crafting?
- What potential job crafting interventions or solutions are available?
- What is the evidence from published research to show how effective job crafting interventions are and whether they are likely to be effective in our organizational context? What is the quality of the evidence?
- What are the potential negative consequences of job crafting?
- How will we evaluate the effects of the intervention?

In Chapter 8 we will explore in more detail what the implications of taking an evidence-based approach would be for job crafting.

Conclusion

As we have explored in this chapter, there are a variety of ways in which people can be directly and indirectly encouraged to personalize their work. These range from formal and specific workshops to informal coaching and encouragement. Ultimately, the best approach to take if an organization wants to encourage job crafting will be based on their context and culture.

A key part of the decision-making process in terms of whether to invest in job crafting will be whether there is an evidence base to do so and the extent to which job crafting aligns with, and supports, the people priorities and HR agenda of a particular organization. These two themes will be the focus of the next chapter.

KEY POINTS

- Job crafting can't be forced but it can be encouraged and stimulated by exercises and activities.
- Job crafting exercises can be undertaken alone, in pairs or in groups.
- It is recommended that job crafting is voluntary rather than mandatory.
- The best job crafting activity to choose will be dependent on your organizational context.

QUESTIONS

- Which activities would you most like to undertake and explore? Why?

- What activities would best suit your team or organization?

- How would you measure the success of the different activities?

Notes

1 Van den Heuvel, M, Demerouti, E and Peeters, M C W (2015) The job crafting intervention: effects on job resources, self-efficacy, and affective well-being, *Journal of Occupational and Organizational Psychology*, 88 (3), pp 511–32, doi: 10.1111/joop.12128

2 Tonhäuser, C and Büker, L (2016) Determinants of transfer of training: a comprehensive literature review, *International Journal for Research in Vocational Education and Training*, 3 (2), pp 127–65

3 Job Crafting Exercise, available at: https://jobcrafting.com/collections/front-page-collection/products/booklet (archived at https://perma.cc/PRG5-4KNB)

4 Schrijver, N (2018) Job crafting, job crafting interventions and their successfulness: a literary review, available at: http://arno.uvt.nl/show.cgi?fid=147431 (archived at https://perma.cc/N9JA-YDKD)

5 Osterwalder, A (2005) What is a business model? *Business Model Alchemist*, available at: http://businessmodelalchemist.com/blog/2005/11/what-is-business-model.html (archived at https://perma.cc/M2BW-KW35)

6 Strauss, K, Griffin, M A and Parker, S K (2012) Future work selves: how salient hoped-for identities motivate proactive career behaviors, *Journal of Applied Psychology*, 97 (3), pp 580–98, doi: 10.1037/a0026423

7 Ibid

8 Strauss, K and Parker, S K (2018) Intervening to enhance proactivity in organizations: improving the present or changing the future, *Journal of Management*, 44 (3), pp 1250–78

9 Baumeister, R F et al (2001) Bad is stronger than good, *Review of General Psychology*, 5 (4), p 323

10 Hone, L C et al (2015) Flourishing in New Zealand workers: associations with lifestyle behaviors, physical health, psychosocial, and work-related indicators, *Journal of Occupational and Environmental Medicine*, 57 (9), pp 973–83

11 Corporate Leadership Council (2002) Building the high-performance workforce, available at: https://marble-arch-online-courses.s3.amazonaws.com/CLC_Building_the_High_Performance_Workforce_A_Quantitative_Analysis_of_the_Effectiveness_of_Performance_Management_Strategies1.pdf (archived at https://perma.cc/CJ6L-L57R)

12 McQuaid, M, Niemiec, R and Doman, F (2018) A character strengths-based approach to positive psychology coaching, *Positive Psychology Coaching in Practice*, pp 71–79

13 McQuaid, M and Lawn, E (2014) *Your Strengths Blueprint: How to be engaged, energized and happy at work*, Michelle McQuaid

14 Leana, C, Appelbaum, E and Shevchuk, I (2009) Work process and quality of care in early childhood education: the role of job crafting, *Academy of Management Journal*, 52 (6), pp 1169–92

15 McClelland, G P *et al* (2014) Collaborative crafting in call centre teams, *Journal of Occupational and Organizational Psychology*, 87 (3), pp 464–86

16 Wrezesniewski, A (2014) Engage in job crafting, in J E Dutton and G M Spreitzer, *How to be a Positive Leader: Small actions, big impact*, Berrett-Koehler Publishers

17 Wingerden, J V and Poell, R F (2017) Employees' perceived opportunities to craft and in-role performance: the mediating role of job crafting and work engagement, *Frontiers in Psychology*, 8 (1876)

18 Briner, R B and Walshe, N D (2015) An evidence-based approach to improving the quality of resource-oriented well-being interventions at work, *Journal of Occupational and Organizational Psychology*, 88 (3), pp 563–86

08

Supporting the HR agenda through job crafting

Whilst the majority of examples and ideas presented in this book have been from a bottom-up, employee-led perspective, this chapter will change the focus slightly towards what HR professionals and senior leaders can do to embed a personalized approach to work from a leadership, work and organizational design perspective. This chapter will specifically include examples of how different organizations have encouraged and enabled people to personalize their work, an overview of how job crafting aligns to different HR people agendas, and evidence-based ideas for how to foster job crafting across an organization.

Taking an evidence-based approach

How can you ensure that job crafting is an initiative that will add value to people within your organization? How can you assure yourself and others that you are clear on what you are hoping to change and improve and the difference you are trying to make? When working with organizations to navigate these types of questions, I advocate using an evidence-based practice approach.

At the heart of evidence-based practice is the notion that sound decisions are achieved through the application of a clear process which involves sourcing, evaluating and working through the best evidence available. Rather than only relying on a few sources of information such as personal experiences, or espoused best practice, evidence-based decision making encourages people to, wherever possible, base their decisions on information and insights collected from a variety of sources. The Centre for Evidence-Based Management (CEBMa)[1] suggests that before making important decisions organizations should follow a formal process including the collection and consideration of distinct types of evidence.

WHY DO WE NEED TO TAKE AN EVIDENCE-BASED APPROACH?

Much as we may not want to believe it, our decisions and judgements are highly susceptible to bias and errors. We may be seduced by a new idea or topic because it aligns with our personal beliefs or be persuaded to take a course of action because it has started to be recognized as 'best and leading practice' within our sector. We are prone to these errors and biases for a number of reasons and in part this is because we have limited cognitive resources and time to make decisions. Consequently (as we explored in Chapter 2) we take natural shortcuts or 'heuristics' to make thinking quicker and easier.

The way we might naturally make decisions is therefore likely to be subject to a number of biases. The thinking of an individual or a group may therefore not be as clear and rational as they would like to believe. For example, people are prone to confirmation bias which means that we – often subconsciously – search for information or evidence which supports our own thoughts or impressions. As well as brain function foibles, biases could creep into decision making in other ways. For example, making decisions solely on what is considered to be best practice is also prone to potential bias. Without critically evaluating how a new idea or policy might work within your organization, you are effectively relying on the 'reported' experiences of other organizations. And in most instances, for various reasons, organizations may be inclined to report and present beneficial results without necessarily showcasing or highlighting the negative results.

Collecting different types of evidence

CEBMa suggest that four sources of information are used to inform decision making: scientific evidence, organizational evidence, experiential evidence and stakeholder evidence.

SCIENTIFIC EVIDENCE
Scientific information refers to published evidence available from academic publications. For those working in HR these publications relate to the fields

of Management, Human Resources, Work and Organizational Psychology. The quality and the relevance of the scientific evidence should always be considered.

From a job crafting perspective, as we explored in Chapter 4, there is a large and growing body of scientific evidence developing from peer-reviewed academic journals. This research has explored the efficacy of job crafting in a number of different professional and organizational contexts and has shown a variety of potential benefits for individuals and businesses. There are of course key limitations to the evidence reported and these include an absence of double-blind randomized controlled research and inconsistencies in the precise definitions and measurements of job crafting being used across studies.

EXAMPLE
Using evidence

The Director for Organizational Development at a UK university was interested in exploring whether job crafting could support the university's career framework. Before making any commitments and decisions, he asked an OD manager to produce a short summary of key evidence and relevant research studies. Collectively, the OD team considered the strengths and weaknesses of job crafting from an empirical basis and specifically the strength of job crafting research which related to careers. Ultimately, it was decided that the science base was sufficient to explore job crafting further with other stakeholders.

ORGANIZATIONAL

A second source of evidence relates to information and insights from the organization itself. Within HR this could relate to data collected from staff surveys or broader information in terms of recruitment, retention and turn-over. Similarly, it could be more specific, such as complaints (or compliments) coming from certain areas of the business or relating to certain organizational issues.

Organizational insights and evidence can help to inform whether there is an issue or problem that needs addressing and, if there is, what will be the most effective way of doing this. Areas where research has indicated that job crafting may have a positive influence include: engagement and satisfaction at work; turnover and retention; flexibility and agility; and change and innovation.

EXAMPLE
Organizational insights

The senior HR team of a national UK bank had been commissioned by the Chief
People Officer to explore ways to encourage people to be able to work more
flexibly. The bank's executive board had requested this in response to
information gathered from a number of sources, including staff surveys, exit
interviews and staff forums on supporting maternity and paternity leave.
Further focus groups run by the HR team identified that one key barrier to
flexible working was a lack of confidence amongst employees and their line
managers about how to approach and deliver their work differently. Job crafting
was identified as one approach which could give employees and their team
leaders a framework and language with which to do this.

PRACTITIONER

A third source of evidence relates to the professional knowledge, judgement
and wisdom of people working within and outside of the organization. These
might include practitioners, managers, consultants or other business leaders.
This specialized knowledge comes from the experiences and insights accu-
mulated through direct experience, learning and critical thought.

When considering whether to explore job crafting and a more personalized approach to work, the views and opinions of practitioners are important.
For example, they will have an understanding of whether job crafting as a
concept or methodology is likely to 'fit' the organizational context and what
level of support and training would be needed to both explain and encourage job crafting in different areas of the business.

EXAMPLE
Practitioner experience

The Chief People Officer of a health and physiotherapy company brought
together a group of people to consider whether or not to explore job crafting as
a means to support an organizational objective to encourage individual and
team innovation. The working group included people from across the
organization. Leaders who had previously worked in environments where
people had been given autonomy and were encouraged to align aspects of their
work with their strengths could understand and see how job crafting could
provide value to the business. Other senior managers in the working group
were more sceptical and expressed concerns about giving people too much
autonomy, particularly in more transactional roles. It was felt that front-facing

roles such as physiotherapists, with very time-constrained jobs in terms of seeing patients and writing up notes, may have fewer opportunities to craft than people in back-office roles. Based on the feedback from the group the Chief People Officer decided to test job crafting and run a small number of evaluated trials with back-office and front-office teams. The results from these pilots were positive and evidence was collected directly and indirectly from participants to demonstrate how they had applied job crafting in their roles.

STAKEHOLDER

A fourth source of evidence comes from the values, beliefs, ideas and concerns of organizational stakeholders. These are any individuals or groups who may be affected by the decisions and consequences of the decisions being made. Internal stakeholders might include employees, leaders and board members. External stakeholders, those outside of the organization, could include customers, suppliers, trade unions and shareholders. Each stakeholder group or individual may have divergent values and beliefs about the significance or consequence of the ideas being considered and the importance of any associated risks or rewards. The views and opinions of stakeholders can therefore be an important frame of reference from which to evaluate and analyse evidence from different sources.

EXAMPLE
Stakeholder perspectives

A cloud-based technology company of 800 employees had just received significant external funding. A new Head of People and Performance role was established to further develop and sustain a work environment that would support the company's vision and commitments for growth and development. Job crafting was seen by a member of the HR team as an approach which would underpin and encourage innovation and proactivity. On presenting the idea to the board, there were concerns raised that employees would craft their roles in ways that would take the company 'off mission' which would potentially jeopardize targets. Whilst the Head of People was confident that job crafting could be introduced in a way that would support rather than impede the attainment of individual and organizational goals, they were clear that the wider endorsement and encouragement of the leadership team and the advisory board was not sufficient to progress the idea. As a consequence, a decision was made to pause plans for the formal testing of job crafting and to reconsider the idea in 12 months' time.

Supporting your organization's people and HR agenda

Any organization will often be juggling a number of people and HR priorities at any one time. This next section will explore how job crafting and a personalized approach to work has the potential to support and add value to 10 different people-related themes, which often sit high on an organization's people and HR agenda. These themes are listed in Table 8.1 and explored individually below.

Change and transformation

Change is constant in most companies. It's caused by a variety of external and internal forces including technological innovation, shifts in strategic objectives, new senior leadership appointments and legislative changes. Yet the truth is that most coordinated attempts to manage change within organizations fail to deliver on their intended purpose and business objectives.[2] In reality, there is no single way to manage change effectively, but there is increasing recognition and evidence that 'big bang' top-down approaches to change fail to deliver.[3] Instead, more adaptive and emergent approaches to change, where people are trusted and enabled to lead iterative

TABLE 8.1 The HR themes directly supported by a job crafting and personalized approach

HR theme	Related HR concepts
Change and transformation	Change, transformation, innovation, development
Employee engagement and motivation	Employee engagement, attraction, recruitment, retention, performance, employee brand, employee experience
Performance	Performance management, productivity
Flexible working	Flexible working, agile working
Making adjustments	Ill-health, maternity leave, paternity leave, positively dealing with disability
Meeting changing workforce needs	Ageing workforce, human-centred design
Health and wellbeing	Mental health, physical health, wellbeing
Diversity and inclusion	Diversity, inclusion, neurodiversity
Coaching	Coaching, line management, team working
Talent	Attraction, recruitment, retention, performance, employee brand

and continuous change and improvement in alignment to a clear organizational direction, are increasingly being recognized as a more effective and responsive approach.[4]

INSIGHT FROM AN HR LEADER – ANDY DODMAN

Andy Dodman, Chief People Officer at Leeds City Council, agrees that job crafting can positively influence change. Andy is recognized as one of the UK's leading HR professionals[5] and in an interview with him about job crafting he told me:

> Change isn't monolithic or linear. It's actually based on human iteration and intervention. Consequently, change doesn't start with a management framework, model or system – it always starts with the individual... and job crafting can play a part in creating an expectation that change can and should come from employees themselves doing something different or working in different ways.

As well as fuelling innovation, collaboration and experimentation, which is critical to more agile approaches to change, job crafting also encourages people and project teams to have clarity about the purpose and impact of the work they are doing for themselves and the wider organization. On an individual basis, job crafting also helps people adjust to, and work with, change effectively. People experience change in different ways, some with excitement and others with dread and disengagement. By shaping their jobs in response to, and in alignment to changes they experience, individuals may be better able to respond to and work with change rather than get swept up and away with it, which often happens. In terms of performance this obviously helps but it is also significant from a wellbeing and health perspective, enabling people to positively respond to and cope with change.

Three specific ways that job crafting supports a more adaptive and agile approach to change are by:

- delivering change and innovation through continuous reflection, improvement and adaption;
- supporting an environment where people are trusted and feel psychologically safe to try new approaches and adapt the way they work;
- enabling employees to use job crafting as a mechanism to cope with the personal challenges and stresses of change.

Engagement and motivation

Organizations with a focus on fostering employee engagement are curious about how to create a work environment where people are inspired and enabled to give their best every day and motivated to be part of the organization's success. There are multiple HR and organizational factors which influence employee engagement including reward, growth and development opportunities, relationships with line managers and colleagues, flexibility and the overall work environment.

In particular, employee engagement and motivation is fuelled by, or is arguably a reflection of, the relationship between the organization and the employee. And, as is the case with any relationship, its strength is based on the trust, transparency, integrity and positive contribution and commitment shown by both parties. As we know, actions speak larger than words, and when an organization openly and actively encourages job crafting it demonstrates that it is genuinely interested, and vested in, both recognizing all employees as unique individuals but also creating a workplace where people can harness their individual talents and strengths.

INSIGHT FROM AN HR LEADER – ANDY DODMAN

According to Andy Dodman, most organizations are not doing enough to understand and encourage people to find ways to bring their personal talents, strengths and interests to the workplace. Andy sees job crafting as one way to enable people to find a personal spark in the way they approach work. He told me:

> Job crafting allows people to bring their full and whole selves to the work they do. Too many employees leave their personal talents and interests at home when they come to work and we need to challenge and stop this. Organizations and their leaders need to encourage people to bring these passions and strengths to the workplace. We need to be telling people, 'please find a way to bring your passions and talents fully to work, it would be brilliant if you do because other people will be inspired by you and we can all learn from your expertise'.

Three ways in which job crafting supports and promotes employee engagement and motivation are by:

- encouraging ways of working that promote autonomy, connection and purpose and energy at work;
- enabling people to bring their diverse, whole and best selves to work;
- creating opportunities for people to explore the meaning and purpose of their work.

Performance

For organizations who are serious and committed to encouraging high performance, job crafting is a compelling approach to enable people to uncover, unlock and fulfil their potential. Job crafting is a positive, purpose-full and strengths-based way of baking autonomy, control and purpose into work. It provides a framework and stimulus for meaningful conversations amongst colleagues and line managers about how to improve jobs and better align activities with the strengths, talents and interests of people, both on an individual basis and across teams. Personalized approaches to work naturally encourage people to reflect on organizational and individual goals and the wider purpose of work. These are all factors which are consistently shown to underpin performance on a sustainable basis.

Leaders, and line managers in particular, are critical in enabling performance. They reinforce and support the links between business and individual objectives and can give clear and pertinent feedback in ways that enable people to remain accountable for how they perform whilst exploring ways to maintain and improve their performance. In order to support job crafting, leaders have to adopt a more supportive and open style of leadership, and create the space and opportunity for growth and experimentation.

INSIGHT FROM AN HR LEADER – JULIA SMITH

Julia Smith, Founder and Director of People Science, has worked with organizations to embed job crafting as an HR Director and also as a consultant. In an interview with Julia, she was clear about the beneficial role that job crafting could play in lifting the quality of both performance conversations and overall performance. She told me:

> Job crafting puts a completely different lens on performance and performance discussions. It enables colleagues and their managers to explore how a job currently aligns with an individual's strengths and talents and identify the small changes and adjustments that can make the job a better fit... it also encourages people to think about and explore the purpose of their work, which fuels motivation and performance, and this is something I personally found really powerful when I explored job crafting myself individually and with my team.

Three ways job crafting can help elements of a performance management and enablement agenda are by:

- aligning people's work with their strengths, passions and interests in ways that drive and support performance;
- embedding a mindset of continuous curiosity and improvement;
- encouraging ways of working that boost autonomy support, which fuels motivation, discretionary effort, innovation and creativity.

Flexible and agile working

Flexibility shouldn't be thought of as part-time working or occasionally working from home. Flexible or agile working gives people agency over the hours, locations and times that they work. Providing opportunities for people to craft and customize their working arrangements enables employees to work when and where they are most productive and able to do their best work.

Job crafting recognizes that one size does not fit all when it comes to the structure and timings of work and empowers people to personalize their working arrangements to find better alignment and harmony in their overall life. Adopting personalized working as a default widens the pool of opportunity for people to find ways to make their most impactful contribution.

For organizations struggling, or aspiring, to transition from fixed and static to more agile and adaptable ways of working, job crafting is one approach which can help to stimulate people to be curious about exploring and shifting their standard working hours, patterns and routines.

Three ways that job crafting can support flexible working are by:

- encouraging people, managers and teams to be more open and flexible in their approach to work – moving away from seeing jobs and work as rigid and static;

- providing individuals and managers with a framework to initiate and structure conversations about how to change the make-up or time component of roles;

- exploring where, when and how people do their best work and encouraging employees to experiment with working in different ways.

Making adjustments and changes to existing roles

In my experience people often struggle to find a mutually satisfying way of agreeing new working patterns and redesigned ways of working because managers, and often the employees themselves, find it hard to break apart, or reshape, their existing jobs. Similarly, many organizations struggle to seamlessly make adjustments in positive ways when someone becomes unable to fulfil an existing element of their job. Too often, in the case of reducing hours, rather than redesign the way work is done, people try to literally compress and squeeze their old ways of working into a narrower time frame. In the case of adjustments to elements of a job, managers often fail to be able to accommodate any changes and just give up and say amendments are not possible. Ultimately, this inability to make adjustments negatively impacts on the individual's ability and motivation to do their job and makes their work more challenging to deliver at a time when they are often facing pressures and challenges from other aspects of their life.

It is possible to respond positively and proactively for requests to make adjustments to roles on a temporary and permanent basis. Job crafting gives managers and individuals a frame of reference and approach to discuss how to make changes that meet the needs of both the individual and the organization. In businesses that have embedded a personalized and flexible approach to work into their culture and structure, adjustments to roles almost become a non-issue. Beyond the need to deal with contract and payroll changes, in a personalized work environment, adjustments to tasks and responsibilities are simply business as usual. They don't require clunky and process-heavy meetings to accommodate change, which is still the norm in many organizations.

Three ways job crafting can help organizations respond to and facilitate requests to make changes and adjustments to roles are by:

- providing both the manager and the individual with an opportunity to reframe how they see a job – rather than a fixed construct it is made up of a number of adaptable components which can be shaped, adapted, amplified or removed;

- giving managers and individuals a language and framework to hold positive and constructive conversations about how to make changes to work on a phased, temporary, or permanent basis;

- providing employees with a way to explore the aspects of work that they enjoy the most, are most meaningful and they are best at.

Meeting changing workforce demographics and needs

The world of work is becoming richer and more age-diverse, with more generations working together than ever before.[6] Whilst much has been written about the divergent motives, values and abilities of different generations, research shows that it's dangerous and complacent to make sweeping generalizations about the characteristics of a specific group. For example, we know that our personalities and preferences constantly change irrespective of our age and not simply when we hit certain generational or age milestones.[7] A personalized, employee-led, approach to working enables organizations to cater for a diversity of employee needs which will present themselves at different periods of our life, including births, deaths (of people and pets), moving house, dealing with personal health issues and caring responsibilities.

One generational reality that is supported by science and research is the need to adjust and adapt to an ageing workforce. For a mixture of reasons including financial necessity, changes to the pension age and good health, people are working longer and retiring later than ever before.[8] This creates opportunities in training, recruitment and retirement support and planning which traditionally many organizations have ignored or treated as problems to be dealt with rather than realities to be positively responded to. For more enlightened organizations, there are a number of benefits of actively engaging and supporting mature employees. These advantages include broadening talent and experience, delivering better customer service by aligning the age of employees with customers and more broadly making workplaces richer by having greater age diversity.

Job crafting has been highlighted by researchers as an effective tool in enabling older workers to adapt their work to suit their skills and capabilities.[9,10] There are two key reasons for this. First, older workers may be more likely to value the opportunity to job craft and use this approach. A 2013 meta-analysis of employee proactivity involving over 36,000 workers found a positive relationship between age and people taking personal initiative in their jobs.[11] One explanation offered for this is that people who have worked for longer are better placed to spot opportunities for change and experimentation. Second, job crafting can be particularly effective for more mature workers as it enables them to iteratively change and adapt their work to meet their changing circumstances. For example, employees who have work which has both physical and technical components (eg mechanics, builders, engineers, laboratory technicians) could craft their role to reduce the physical components of their work and increase training or technical elements which would make the most use of their skills, knowledge and expertise.

Job crafting and a personalized approach to work can support an age-diverse workforce by:

- supporting growth for life – enabling people to reflect on ways to grow and develop throughout all stages of their working life;
- providing individuals and managers with a tool to identify, adapt and craft their work in ways that best suit their personal needs and interests;
- being a positive approach to frame conversations and discussions about how to meet the changing needs and capacities of an age-diverse workforce.

Health and wellbeing

Looking after people's health and wellbeing is simply the right thing to do. Increasingly, organizations are recognizing this moral imperative, but also the wider tangential benefits of having a more energized and healthier workforce. It is therefore not surprising that designing work and creating workplace experiences which foster wellbeing are increasingly being reported as being high on the agenda of HR teams and executive boards.[12]

There is a wealth of evidence which we have explored throughout this book that demonstrates the compelling connection between job crafting and positive health and wellbeing. Personalized job design which enables people to craft autonomy, control and connection into their work should be a foundational component of any holistic organizational wellbeing agenda.

INSIGHT FROM AN HR LEADER – ANDY DODMAN

Wellbeing means different things to different people. It's individual and personal. An organization can't define or dictate for an individual what their wellbeing is and isn't, but it can invite and encourage people to explore what will make the biggest difference to their own personal wellbeing and then do everything it can to allow them to find and fulfil this.

Connection and community are two areas I believe are particularly important in fostering wellbeing and people can craft their work to find ways to share their passions and interests with others – for example holding or attending a book club, starting a choir or a lunchtime running club... there are so many talents and interests that reside within our workforces and a mistake organizations often make is to ignore people's interests which don't, on the surface, appear to align to work. But these interests can be used as a focal point to bring people together, to create collaborations and foster connections, which will ultimately benefit the wider organization in both tangible and intangible ways.

Specifically, three ways that job crafting could support a health and wellbeing agenda are by:

- enabling people to shape and adapt their work to meet short- or long-term physical and mental health challenges;
- promoting ways of working that are strongly related to positive wellbeing – this enables people to take greater control and autonomy of their work, and drives job satisfaction and alignment with individual purpose and values;
- providing individuals and managers with a mechanism to better balance their work demands and resources – this might include dialling up or down certain aspects of work, finding and creating opportunities to re-energize at work and shaping how, where, and when work is done which best aligns to an individual's needs.

Diversity and inclusion

Businesses with a commitment to diversity and inclusion value everyone as an individual. Creating an inclusive workplace enables every employee to fully participate and reach their potential. We all benefit from embracing and valuing the rich diversity of thoughts, skills and strengths that people bring to a company which stem from the different experiences, backgrounds and identities we all have. An inclusive people approach which celebrates and nurtures diversity boosts learning and development, improves decision making, fosters innovation and allows organizations to meet the varied needs of their customers.

At the heart of job crafting and personalized working is the recognition that we are all different. It encourages individuals, leaders and organizations to be curious about people's idiosyncrasies and find ways to harness and recognize these to create value and contribution.

INSIGHT FROM AN HR LEADER – JULIA SMITH

At the core of any inclusion strategy is enabling people to bring their whole selves to their work. For me, job crafting is the embodiment of this. Job crafting can be a powerful tool in helping to explore how people show up at work and how to embody and express passions, strengths, life experiences and interests to make work more meaningful, purposeful and stimulating. If organizations can create and stimulate an environment where people can do this, then this is a genuinely inclusive approach to work.

Job crafting provides a mechanism to enable people to individually and collaboratively explore, harness and amplify their talents, strengths and interests in their work. Specifically, three ways that job crafting can support a diversity and inclusion agenda are by:

- encouraging conversations and activities which positively recognize individuality, neurodiversity and different experiences, thoughts, skills, identities and backgrounds;
- unlocking the unique and individual strengths, talents and interests that we all have;
- enabling people to bring their full, whole and best self to work.

Coaching

Creating coaching opportunities for employees is an increasingly popular approach in organizations seeking to support performance and more broadly leadership, career and skills development. Coaching creates the space, and provides a framework for people to develop their own thinking and actions towards a target or goal and helps them identify the specific skills and strengths they need to harness and develop to get them there. HR and people-led functions have a key role in encouraging coaching and specifically the different coaching styles, approaches and interventions which will work best, for both their employees and the business as a whole.

Job crafting supports a coaching approach as it is employee-led and personalized to the needs of the individual. As well as using external specialist job crafting coaches, managers and team leaders can be internally trained to support coaching discussions which have a focus on how to enable an individual to create a stronger personal job fit by personalizing, re-framing and shaping their job activities, relationships and working practices.

INSIGHT FROM AN HR LEADER – JULIA SMITH

For me, job crafting has the potential to be a powerful coaching tool. It provides team leaders with a positive and supportive framework to have conversations with colleagues about their jobs and what they do on a day-to-day basis. It puts employees and their thoughts and feelings at the heart of the conversation and enables employees to generate their own ideas about how to fulfil more of their potential and how to make their work more personal, tailored and ultimately more effective.

Three ways that job crafting supports an organization's coaching agenda are by:

- encouraging exploration of, and self-awareness about, strengths, skills and values;
- creating opportunities for people to think critically and curiously about how they do their work – including their tasks, relationships, purpose and how their work relates to their wellbeing;
- enabling and trusting people to have agency and proactivity to shape their jobs.

Talent enhancement

HR and people professionals have a key role to play in designing, developing and supporting a talent management approach which aligns with the business needs of their organization. Effective talent management approaches can create learning organizations, consolidate an employer's brand as an 'employer of choice' and help to unlock employee potential and create sustainable opportunities for progression and career development. Given this list, it is perhaps not surprising that talent management is an area of increasing priority for organizations, with the CIPD finding that over half of chief executives identify talent management as an area of strategic priority, focus and investment.[13]

In terms of development and career progression, job crafting can be used as a mechanism to enable people to fulfil their potential and make a long-term difference to their organization. In particular, job crafting encourages people to understand their current skills, strengths and interests and to consider how these can be broadened, deepened or refocused to meet their aspirations. Broadening perspectives and lifting people's attention towards the future may make them better able to spot opportunities across the organization when they present themselves or, if they don't exist, to craft or create them.

INSIGHT FROM AN HR LEADER – JESSICA AMORTEGUI

As Jessica Amortegui, Director of Executive Development at LinkedIn, told me:

> Traditional approaches to talent development are broken... people waste their time looking for perfect jobs, when in reality are they are like unicorns, they don't exist. Instead, through job crafting, people can intelligently cultivate work to reflect their individuality to create the best possible fit with their talents, strengths and interests.

This approach benefits both the individual and the organization. Jessica goes on to explain:

> Rather than looking outside of their current jobs for their next challenge, job crafting enables people to realize the latent potential for development within their existing jobs.

Three ways that job crafting can support talent management are by:

- aligning work to people's personal strengths and passions – to boost performance and foster job satisfaction, engagement and ultimately retention;

- enabling people to take greater ownership and control of their personal growth and career progression;
- creating opportunities for individuals and teams to reflect on their diverse skills and talents and how they align to current and future business priorities.

Creating job crafting organizations

Whilst job crafting is typically a solo or small team endeavour, this does not mean that organizations, and leaders in particular, have no role to play in supporting job crafting. There are a number of ways that HR, organizational leaders and line managers can help to facilitate job crafting that directly support the strategic and operational ambitions of the organization. These include boosting autonomy, being clear on purpose and mission, taking development conversations to the next level, creating slack, and promoting psychological safety.

Boosting autonomy

Fundamentally, when people feel that they have genuine autonomy, trust and discretion in how they undertake their jobs and execute their work, they are more likely to craft and customize their jobs. These factors are often in the direct control of leaders and for this reason they are often critical in encouraging or inhibiting job crafting. Dr Gavin Slemp from the Centre of Positive Psychology at the University of Melbourne studies job crafting and leadership. Through his research Dr Slemp has found that leadership style is an important factor in influencing the amount and type of job crafting people undertake.

There is one specific leadership style in particular that Dr Slemp believes positively encourages job crafting as well as providing wider benefits to both employees and their organization. As he explained to me, 'Leaders with a style which researchers refer to as "autonomy supportive" can boost job crafting'. These leaders are more likely to let employees control the direction of their work and only intervene when asked or when it is critical to do so. Leaders who boost autonomy and the personalization of work tend to focus more on outcomes than the minutia of how work is done. Dr Slemp told me, 'By focusing on the ends for which people are responsible whilst relaxing the management of the means of how work is done, team leaders increase the likelihood that people will craft their roles'.

As well as supporting job crafting specifically, the broader benefits of an autonomous leadership style are considerable. A 2018 global meta-analysis of over 30,000 people, led by Dr Slemp with colleagues, found that leaders who actively promoted and encouraged autonomous working fostered intrinsic motivation amongst employees, which in turn was linked to greater workplace wellbeing, proactive behaviour, engagement and performance.[14] Dr Slemp confirmed, 'When leaders have an autonomous supportive style, their employees are more likely to feel that their individual and motivational needs are being met'. The benefits of this type of leadership do not appear to be related to specific global territories or cultural domains. Dr Slemp told me, 'The results from across the world suggested to the research team that autonomous supportive leadership is something that is valued everywhere, and tends to enable positive outcomes wherever it is practised.'

Whilst some leaders may naturally adopt a trusting, supportive and autonomous style this sadly isn't the approach that everyone takes. Dr Slemp believes that training and coaching could be effective for some managers, particularly those who are receptive to learn about their leadership style and maybe don't realize that their current approach is not as supportive and effective as it could be.

As well as top-down coaching, leadership styles can also be influenced by feedback from colleagues and through his research, Dr Slemp has specifically observed subordinate employees crafting more autonomy support into their leaders. As he explained to me:

> Through some of our research we have seen that employees can actively develop
> and build their relationship with their boss to the extent that they can shape
> how their manager treats them. For example, the employee might give feedback
> that they appreciated the trust the manager showed them in letting them lead
> a project without their involvement, or valued that their boss let them try
> something new, and take a small risk in how work is being done.

Whilst feedback to leaders can be effective, there is no guarantee that this will always result in effective and lasting change. It can be easier to influence some people than others and certain leaders may simply be too tethered to traditional command and control models of management to change their approach. Ultimately, an organization, shaped by the thoughts and influence of HR, needs to decide which leadership approaches and styles best serve their employees, their organization and their customers and find ways to support, tackle, and even remove, people who are unable or unwilling to support this style.

There are a number of ways in which organizations and leaders can shift to a more autonomous supportive approach. Pulling together research and practice, Dr Gavin Slemp and Lara Mossman have highlighted behaviours which signify a reflect a more supportive and employee-focused leadership style.[15] These include:

- creating opportunities for people to make their own work choices;

- enabling people to input into decision making;

- trusting people to use their own discretion in how work is done and making decisions about their work;

- showing an active interest in the ideas, thoughts and perspectives of their colleagues;

- encouraging ownership of individual goals;

- reinforcing and promoting the value of the work and tasks being undertaken by their team;

- celebrating and highlighting achievements and milestones reached by team members; and

- avoiding being overly controlling or micro-managing.

To what extent do you adopt these behaviours? And what about your colleagues? This is a useful checklist to compare and contrast against your own leadership style and the approach of leaders across your organization.

Be clear on purpose and mission

From a job crafting perspective, having a clear purpose and mission is important for a number of reasons. First, it gives employees a 'north star' with which to focus their job crafting activities and to ensure that when they customize their work, they move towards, rather than away from, the strategic direction of the business. Second, a clear mission and purpose enables people to understand the value and purpose of the work they are doing which helps with more meaning, purpose and cognitive-focused types of job crafting.

The worth of mission and vision statements can be measured by the extent to which they are 'lived and breathed' by the organizations. Employees are quick to spot inauthentic 'why washing' where the motivation to develop purpose and mission statements appears to be for branding reasons rather than a genuine desire to distil and communicate what the organization stands for and believes in.

A powerful way for organizations to demonstrate that they truly believe in their mission and purpose is to share stories about how employees bring their values to life. Zappos, a US online retailer, is a company that does this well. Its customer service levels are legendary and it is fully and wholly committed to its organizational mission of 'Delivering happiness to customers, employees and vendors'.[16] Rather than give its customer service and call centre teams strict targets for how quickly they respond to and terminate a customer call, Zappos empowers and trusts their colleagues to spend as much time as they feel is warranted to create the exceptional customer experience that they are committed to. In 2016, Steven Weinstein, working in the Zappos customer loyalty team, set a company record for the longest customer call of an amazing 10 hours and 43 minutes. When interviewed about the call, he said that he sees it as part of his role and part of the Zappos ethos to develop connections and even friendships with customers.[17] This call was deemed by Zappos as a cause for celebration. They wanted people inside and outside of the organization to know that they really valued and believed in their mission to deliver extraordinary service.

To support job crafting which fosters a sense of meaning and aligns with an organization's purpose, leaders can actively reinforce the importance and significance of the work that people do. Here are three ideas for doing this:

- **Let purpose be an invisible leader** – Zach Mercurio, author and researcher on purpose and meaningfulness, suggests that organizations treat their mission and purpose as if it was a key stakeholder in making a decision.[18] A question that leaders should ask and discuss with colleagues is, 'What would our purpose have to say about this?' This allows people to avoid getting caught up in, and distracted by, making short-term decisions and noise that could compromise and interfere with the integrity of the business and instead focus more intentionally on long-term and sustainable impact.

- **Close the gap between employee and the end user** – too often people don't have opportunities to connect with, and understand how their work adds value to, their customers. This can be achieved by regularly creating opportunities to hear directly or indirectly from end users, allowing employees to tangibly and directly see and feel how their work matters.

- **Encourage discussions around purpose** – rather than assume that purpose is something that employees think about, leaders and managers can encourage and create opportunities for people to reflect on and discuss the impact they are making and the value of their work to others.

Taking development conversations to the next level

Supportive leaders recognize that most employees naturally seek, and are motivated by, opportunities to develop themselves as individuals at the same time as working to fulfil the aims and ambitions of their organization. To enable and support personal growth, many organizations encourage development discussions between team leaders and the people they manage. These focused conversations provide opportunities for employees to explore their ambitions and how to progress their roles and careers. Typically, these take place through scheduled meetings at set times during the year or, more informally, during the course of check-ins or one-to-one conversations.

As well as reflecting on longer-term career goals, development discussions are an ideal opportunity to include job crafting conversations where people are encouraged to reflect on how they can improve the design and delivery of their job and the small changes they can identify and test to make their work even better. By facilitating and encouraging these types of discussions, organizations are demonstrating to employees that they are interested in, and committed to, their personal development and growth. Connect Health are an example of an organization that has reinvented its performance and development discussions in this way and has embedded job crafting into the fabric of the organization. A case study outlining their approach is provided at the end of this chapter.

Michaela Schoberova is HR Director at a global consumer products company based in the US. She discovered job crafting through her postgraduate studies in positive psychology and has written about how job crafting can be used in development planning and discussions to support employees and managers in co-crafting and creating meaningful and productive work.[19] Co-crafting in this way encourages employees to develop job crafting goals in partnership with their managers. Speaking to Michaela, she describes the benefits of this approach:

> Both the employee and the line manager benefit when they collectively discuss job crafting goals. An employee gains the support and encouragement from their manager to craft their work in meaningful and positive ways and the manager ensures that the employee develops and crafts their job in alignment with the goals of the organization.

In our discussions Michaela highlighted that there are a number of synergies between traditional career development planning and collaborative job crafting. These include a shared focus on:

- change, growth and the maximization of personal potential;
- increasing self-reflection and self-awareness – particularly in relation to personal strengths and talents;
- employee-led ideas, goals and targets which are then shaped with input from the manager.

In terms of barriers, Michaela recognizes that the quality of the conversation between the manager and individual will be critical in determining the impact of the co-crafting discussions and is realistic that some individuals and managers will find the process easier than others. Michaela told me, 'You can't force people to job craft, and some people might struggle more than others to identify meaningful goals'. One positive step organizations can take is to invest in high-quality training, guidance and support for both managers and employees to help them through the process. This gives managers the confidence, skills and knowledge to embed job crafting conversations into day-to-day or more structured discussions.

Create space and time through slack

As a child, I remember playing with plastic puzzles which involved moving small tiles around a fixed frame to create a picture. The challenge was to jumble up the picture and then to create the original image again. You did this by sliding the tiles up and down and side to side. In order for the puzzle to work you needed to have one tile missing to create the space for the other tiles to move. If you didn't have the gap, there would be no space or opportunity to play with the arrangement of the tiles. Unfortunately, this is often the challenge we present to people in our organizations – we expect people to solve problems and innovate without creating the space and time to do so.

Fundamentally, if we don't create the time to explore how our jobs are designed and performed, or create the space to experiment with new ideas, we will never be able to innovate and personalize our positions. Rather than expecting employees to carve out the space and time to craft their job roles, people leaders and HR professionals need to incorporate space by design. Many, if not most managers are naturally suspicious of slack and treat any unfilled time as a missed opportunity for output and productivity.

Perhaps the most well-known example of an organization building slack and space into its work design is Google. In their 2004 Initial Public Offering letter to prospective stock investors,[20] founders Larry Page and Sergey Brin stated: 'We encourage our employees, in addition to their regular projects, to spend 20 per cent of their time working on what they will think will most benefit Google... this empowers them to be more creative and innovative.' Some of the projects and ideas that have come from what came to be known as '20 per cent time' included GoogleMaps and Gmail. In reality, Google didn't strictly enforce or mandate '20 per cent time' and it is not something that they currently promote. As Lazlo Bock, the former Senior Vice President of People at Google, explained in his book *Work Rules*,[21] there were no policies or regulations surrounding the concept. He writes: 'In some ways, the idea of 20 per cent time is more important than the reality of it'. Ultimately, the significance and value of '20 per cent time' was not the specified time allowance, but the broader permission for people at Google to take time to follow their own ideas and instincts and to collaborate with others in spontaneous and self-directed ways.

Creating and protecting space is perhaps the ultimate sign of commitment by an organization that it wants to stimulate an environment that will enable people to operate at their best, and values the ideas and quality of work that employees will be able to sustainably achieve. Rather than seeing slack or space as a cost, organizations need to see this as an investment in human potential and a source of competitive advantage which can fuel innovation, creativity and ultimately productivity. You don't have to be an inventor or engineer to benefit from space and time to think and reflect. These are two commodities that are so valuable and important that we should be making them available to each and every employee. As HR leaders, we need to work with colleagues to create opportunities for critical reflection, experimentation and innovation. Rather than thinking of slack and space as a distraction from performance, we need to think of it as a component part of performance itself.

Here are four ideas for to how to build more space and time into work:

1 **Invest in employees so they can invest in themselves.** Allocating and expecting that everyone across the organization takes designated time off for personal development without stipulating what or how this time needs to be used. Some examples of organizations that are being proactive about learning and development include Buffer, LinkedIn and Thoughtbot. Buffer[22] has self-development as a core organizational value and encourages people to take time for regular development. They provide free access to reading resources and training, learning groups, and 'professional development Fridays' where people can take half a day for professional development

when they have finished core tasks. LinkedIn have 'InDays' which give employees a day to focus on themselves, the company and the world.[23] In a podcast interview with Eat Sleep Work Repeat,[24] Thoughtbot, a product and digital design company, confirmed that they don't do client-facing work on Fridays and instead people are encouraged to work on whatever activities they feel are the most useful and valuable; this could include anything from learning or refining a new skill to charity outreach and volunteering work.

2 **Encourage breaks.** Encourage people to take intentional restorative breaks during the day. These breaks should be detached and untethered from work and could include taking a walk, spending time outside, having a tea or coffee away from the screen or even a nap. Breaks have been found to be linked to lower burnout and increased levels of focus memory and productivity.[25] When the retailer Staples found that more than 25 per cent of its employees didn't take any breaks, they took active steps to understand what would encourage people to take more rest periods. Two key changes they made were to create more and better break spaces and to give access to better-quality snacks and refreshments, both of which were designed to give people more of an incentive to take a break.[26]

3 **Hackathons.** Also known as hack days or hack fests, hackathons typically involve people from across the organization taking a break from their normal tasks and responsibilities and working collaboratively on a problem or task, usually for an intense period lasting from one to five days. These events provide an opportunity to step away from traditional day-to-day working and thinking and create tremendous potential for innovation and growth as well as networking and learning. Whilst traditionally the domain of technology departments, hackathons can be used across organizations and professional functions. Northumbria Water, for example, hold an annual Innovation Festival which brings together employees, customers, researchers and professional specialists to 'come up with innovative solutions to some of the biggest and hard-hitting challenges faced by society and the environment.'[27] HR can certainly benefit from hackathons and they provide a fantastic opportunity to ideate and prototype new ideas and solutions.

4 **Design jobs with space built in.** There is a natural tendency to design and create jobs on a full-time-equivalent basis of say 35–45 hours a week. We typically over-fill our jobs with tasks and responsibilities and remove any chance and opportunity for people to take on additional projects or

responsibilities or make changes to how work is undertaken. A different approach would be to deliberately 'under-fill' jobs by design, for example creating jobs that could be done in say 20–30 hours a week. Effectively, doing this would be giving every job a 'to be confirmed' (TBC) section. Employees could then decide how to focus the 'free' portion of their work, which could be doing more of their core duties, project work, or simply not working at all and working reduced hours. It would enable and encourage regular conversations with managers about what they would like to do in the 'free' element of their job. An example of a company that does this already is software design and process consultants Menlo Innovations.[28] They restrict any consultant from committing themselves to more than 32 hours a week. This creates an eight-hour buffer during the week for development, planning and other activities.

Psychological safety

If you want people to try new things and actively encourage employees to experiment with ways to make their work better, then it is vital to foster psychological safety. Psychological safety describes an environment where people are comfortable to take sensible risks and where failure is not interpreted as negligence but a sign of growth, learning and experimentation.[29]

In a psychologically supportive and safe environment people are not afraid to show vulnerability, take risks, fail and speak up. These are all factors which are also important in encouraging people to openly job craft. A quality job crafting conversation with a manager will entail a colleague being honest about the areas of work they like and dislike, their strengths and passions, the relationships that are working well and those that aren't, opportunities for growth and progression and personal passions and interests. These are all, by their nature, personal to the individual and employees need to feel comfortable trusting their manager to use this information constructively. By design, job crafting involves a form of risk taking and experimentation. People don't always know what the outcome of the change they are making is going to be. As a consequence, people need to feel comfortable that any failures when job crafting will be recognized by their colleagues and their line manager as a misstep or mistake made with the best of intentions. Lastly, the ability to speak up and challenge is important when exploring job crafting because colleagues need to be confident in raising concerns or giving feedback if a teamworker's attempts to craft – perhaps by stopping or changing certain tasks – are having a negative impact.

Here are three ideas to promote and model psychological safety:

1 **Frame future challenges as opportunities for growth and learning.** Rather than set an expectation that future work projects or challenges need to be delivered perfectly first time, leaders can encourage colleagues to recognize these circumstances as an opportunity for growth and learning. By framing work in this way, people are more likely to ask for advice and support and be curious about why things are done in certain ways. By contrast, by setting an expectation that work is something that the team should be able to easily pick up and already know how to do, colleagues are less likely to show vulnerability or a lack of confidence. They are consequently more likely to fear failing the task and less likely to ask questions or seek support. From a job crafting perspective, an expectation of perfection might stifle motivations to craft, particularly if an individual wants to craft in a direction that involves exploring something new and unknown such as volunteering to lead a new work initiative or lead a team for the first time.

2 **Normalize failure.** Failure is part of the learning process. Innovation often involves missteps and mistakes along the way. Leaders can normalize failure by sharing their own mistakes or limitations, for example, in the case of job crafting, by sharing where their attempts to shape their work have not gone as planned. By doing this they are signalling to others that failure is not a form of weakness, but a sign of progression. At Innocent Foods,[30] the founders encouraged their employees to take careful and calculated risks and to learn from and share failures and mistakes when they were made. The leadership team modelled this behaviour by sharing failures and mistakes in newsletters and all staff briefings.

3 **Demonstrate curiosity.** One reason that people don't ask questions within organizations is that they worry that others will judge them negatively for admitting that they don't know all the answers. To encourage people to be more open about what they do and don't know, leaders themselves can model and demonstrate curiosity by asking smart questions. Not only does this promote personal learning, it visibly and powerfully demonstrates to the team that people are not expected to know all the answers, irrespective of their background or experience. For example, if an organizational policy needs to be changed because of new case law or legislation, the leader could ask team members to explain the changes to them. This demonstrates two things: first, the leader wants to learn, and second, the leader does not have all the knowledge or answers.

Conclusion

The time and energy of people at work is finite and too precious to be wasted. Taking a structured and evidence-based approach to decision making is one approach that will help. Wherever possible and appropriate, combining and considering multiple strands of evidence collected from different sources can support HR and people leaders to make investments and provide development and resources which have the best chance of success and make a sustained positive impact on both people and their productivity.

One of the key considerations that should surface through a structured and evidence-based discussion is whether an idea or initiative supports the HR, people and business ambitions of the organization. As we've seen in this chapter, a more individualized and personalized approach to working directly supports a number of current and emerging priorities for HR professional and people leaders. If organizations are serious about taking a holistic, impactful and sustainable approach to areas such as wellbeing, talent development, innovation and performance, then I would argue that it's not possible to do this without focusing on the factors that enable people to find and develop their own ways of working and best meet their current and future needs, strengths and ambitions.

If a decision is made to encourage job crafting, there are a number of areas it is important for HR and leaders to be aware of which enable and encourage people to personalize their work. First, people need the time and space to explore job crafting and this is why some element of slack within the working day or week is so important. This ensures people have the energy and opportunity to shape their work. Second, employees need confidence and encouragement to explore job crafting and factors such as psychological safety and autonomy support. Opportunities to connect with managers through high-quality development conversations become vital to the sustainable success of a personalized approach to working. This is not to say that job crafting can't be encouraged, or won't be possible, without any or all of these aspects being present. But the chances are the job crafting you see will more likely come in the form of trickles rather than torrents and from certain individuals and teams rather than from across the whole organization.

The next (and final) chapter will explore the concept of employee experience, what a truly personalized and exceptional employee experience looks like now, and how it might change in the future.

KEY POINTS

- Organizations should consider the evidence base before implementing any job crafting intervention.
- Job crafting and a personalized approach to work directly supports a number of key HR and leadership priorities including change and transformation, flexible working, wellbeing, performance and talent development.
- Leadership styles which promote autonomous ways of working and psychological safety are particularly effective at enabling job crafting.
- People need time and space to job craft and HR and people leaders should consider how they create and protect this for people within their organizations.

QUESTIONS

- Would a more personalized approach to working support your organization's HR priorities?
- What are the leadership style and behaviours that you foster and promote within your organization? Are they supportive or restrictive of a personalized approach to working?
- How comfortable are people with sharing and expressing failure and taking risks within your organization?
- How do you ensure that people have the time and space for reflection, innovation and experimentation?

CASE STUDY
Connect Health – taking development conversations to the next level

Connect Health is the UK's number one provider of quality muscular skeletal physiotherapy. They partner with a range of organizations including the NHS and private businesses to provide physiotherapy and pain management services. As an organization, Connect Health are committed to creating a work environment where people can bring their full and best selves to work. Recognizing that the relationship between a line manager and an employee is key to this, Connect Health wanted to reframe and re-energize conversations between team leaders and their colleagues.

Moving away from yearly appraisals in 2019, Connect Health introduced opportunities for more regular check-ins and feedback, supported by quarterly one-to-one job crafting discussions. This new approach is called 'Bee Who You Want to Be' and at the heart of the initiative is the invitation and encouragement for everyone working at Connect Health to personalize their jobs in ways that enable them to bring their passions, talents and interests to life. As well as exploring ideas from employees about how to improve the design and delivery of their jobs, team leaders discuss the support that individuals may need to do this, both from them as leaders and from the business more widely.

Every three months, managers are encouraged to have a short job craft-themed discussion with their colleagues. The focus of this discussion varies from quarter to quarter and is aligned to different job crafting elements including tasks and skills, wellbeing, relationships and performance. Whilst team leaders can shape the conversations with their colleagues in the way they feel most appropriate, suggested questions and activities have been provided by the HR team to support both the managers and the individuals. For example, under the wellbeing theme individuals are encouraged to consider questions with their managers such as: 'How does your work influence your health and wellbeing?' 'What does an exceptional day at work look like for you?' and 'What changes to your work would most positively influence your wellbeing?'

For Lisa Davidson, Connect Health's Chief People Officer, job crafting underpins and enables innovation and creativity which is critical to the organization's continued growth and progression. Fundamentally, creating an environment where people can harness and bring their strengths and passions to work is simply seen by Connect Health's Executive Board as the right thing to do, but it is also recognized as a source of competitive advantage in terms of individual and organizational performance and as a positive factor in the attraction, recruitment and retention of passionate and skilled professionals.

Notes

1 Barends, E, Rousseau, D and Briner, R (2014) Evidence-based management: the basic principals, *CEBMa*, available at: https://www.cebma.org/wp-content/uploads/Evidence-Based-Practice-The-Basic-Principles.pdf (archived at https://perma.cc/PMA8-ZY9U)

2 CIPD (2015) Landing transformational change: Closing the gap between theory and practice, available at: https://www.cipd.co.uk/Images/landing-transformation-change_2015-gap-theory-practice_tcm18-9050.pdf (archived at https://perma.cc/M3QJ-DNCR)

3 Ibid

4 Denning, S (2018) *The Age of Agile: How smart companies are transforming the way work gets done*, Amacom

5 HR Magazine (2019) HR Most Influential 2019, available at: http://hrmagazine.co.uk/hr-most-influential/2019-results (archived at https://perma.cc/Q2TV-CLCP)

6 CIDP (2015) Developing the next generation, available at: https://www.cipd.co.uk/Images/developing-next-generation_tcm18-10268.pdf (archived at https://perma.cc/K2KF-8QAT)

7 Harris, M A *et al* (2016) Personality stability from age 14 to age 77 years, *Psychology and Aging*, **31** (8), p 862

8 CIPD (2018) The impact of an ageing workforce, available at: https://www.cipd.co.uk/news-views/cipd-voice/issue-16/impact-ageing-workforce (archived at https://perma.cc/5QHP-XRK9)

9 Nagy, N, Johnston, C and Hirschi, A (2019) Do we act as old as we feel? An examination of subjective age and job crafting behaviour of late career employees, *European Journal of Work and Organizational Psychology*, **28**, 373–83

10 Atkinson, C (Forthcoming) Flexible working for older workers in (eds) S Norgate and C Cooper, *Flexible Work: Designing our healthier future lives*, Abingdon: Taylor and Francis

11 Tornau, K and Frese, M (2013) Construct clean-up in proactivity research: a meta-analysis on the nomological net of work-related proactivity concepts and their incremental validities, *Applied Psychology: An International Review*, **62**, pp 44–96

12 CIPD (2019) Health and well-being at work, available at: https://www.cipd.co.uk/Images/health-and-well-being-at-work-2019.v1_tcm18-55881.pdf (archived at https://perma.cc/M42K-AKPX)

13 CIPD (2017) Resources and talent planning 2017, available at: https://www.cipd.co.uk/Images/resourcing-talent-planning_2017_tcm18-23747.pdf (archived at https://perma.cc/8LXN-SWM7)

14 Slemp, G R *et al* (2018) Leader autonomy support in the workplace: a meta-analytic review, *Motivation and Emotion*, **42** (5), pp 706–24

15 Slemp. G and Mossman, L (2018) Want to lead self-motivated employees? *Pursuit*, available at: https://pursuit.unimelb.edu.au/articles/want-to-lead-self-motivated-employees (archived at https://perma.cc/E5P2-V5MG)

16 Zappos (2009) CEO letter, available at: https://www.zappos.com/ceoletter (archived at https://perma.cc/8QGF-3SJ7)

17 Teemer, A V (2018) This phone rep bonded with a customer for 10 hours, Zappos, available at: https://www.zappos.com/about/stories/record-call (archived at https://perma.cc/XF96-UCQY)

18 McQuaid, M (nd) Podcast with Zach Mercurio, available at: https://www.michellemcquaid.com/podcast/washing-purpose-podcast-zach-mecurio/ (archived at https://perma.cc/T4XD-PCQ9)

19 Schoberova, M (2015) Job crafting and personal development in the workplace: employees and managers co-creating meaningful and productive work in personal development discussions, Master of Applied Positive Psychology (MAPP) Capstone Projects, Paper 87

20 Alphabet Investor Relations (2004) 2004 Founder's IPO letter, available at: https://abc.xyz/investor/founders-letters/2004-ipo-letter/ (archived at https://perma.cc/Y96S-NHH6)

21 Bock, L (2016) *Work Rules!: How Google is changing the way we live and work*, Vahlen

22 Griffis, H (2017) Why we decided to give all employees $20 per month for learning and development, Buffer, available at: https://open.buffer.com/learning-stipend/ (archived at https://perma.cc/22YN-6GWF)

23 McQueen, N (2015) InDay: Investing in our employees so they can invest in themselves, *LinkedIn*, available at: https://blog.linkedin.com/2015/07/29/inday-investing-in-our-employees-so-they-can-invest-in-themselves (archived at https://perma.cc/L5KU-KGKE)

24 Eat Sleep Work Repeat [podcast] (nd) Bringing purpose and autonomy to work, available at: https://podcasts.apple.com/gb/podcast/bringing-purpose-and-autonomy-to-work/id1190000968?i=1000414151973&mt=2 (archived at https://perma.cc/TYP9-SKJM)

25 Ariga, A and Lleras, A (2011) Brief and rare mental 'breaks' keep you focused: deactivation and reactivation of task goals preempt vigilance decrements, *Cognition*, **118** (3), pp 439–43

26 Staples (nd) Staples survey reveals many employees feel too guilty to take breaks, despite spending longer hours at work, available at: http://investor.staples.com/phoenix.zhtml?c=96244&p=irol-newsArticle&ID=1928035&highlight= (archived at https://perma.cc/GY36-NL6R)

27 NWG Innovation Festival, available at: https://innovationfestival.org/ (archived at https://perma.cc/CX5R-LT9Q)

28 Morgan, J W (nd) The joy of lean innovation: a case study of Menlo Innovations, *Lean Enterprises Institute*, available at: https://www.lean.org/Downloads/LPPD2_case_Menlo.pdf (archived at https://perma.cc/H5NN-CKUS)

29 McQuaid, M (nd) Is your team safe? Available at: https://www.michellemcquaid.com/is-your-team-safe/ (archived at https://perma.cc/4RZ9-YNF4)

30 Engage for Success (2014) Case study: employee engagement at South Tees NHS Trust, available at: https://engageforsuccess.org/case-study-employee-engagement-at-south-tees-nhs-trust (archived at https://perma.cc/F3DW-QMNX)

PART FOUR

Embed

09

A personalized people experience for now and the future

In this closing chapter we will explore why and how a personalized people or employee experience can enable both individuals and organizations to flourish as we enter a new era of working heralded by artificial intelligence, automation and robotics. We are in a liminal space where the decisions and choices we make about how we harness and deploy technology will make a profound and lasting difference to our physical and mental wellbeing and all aspects of our personal and working lives.

An exceptional employee experience

Throughout this book, evidence and case examples of how and why job crafting can benefit employees, teams and organizations as a whole have been provided. In Chapter 3, I introduced a job crafting model illustrating the 'why', 'what' and 'how' of job crafting, and at the centre of this is what I believe to be the core benefits of job crafting – thriving, growth and performance. This is shown in Figure 9.1.

Pulling together all the different strands and benefits of job crafting and a personalized approach to work, I believe, fundamentally, that it can provide the foundation for an exceptional people experience within an organization.

An employee, or person, experience (sometimes referred to as EX or PX) captures what people feel about, observe and encounter during their time at work. It spans our first encounters with an organization, from the first time we see and respond to a job vacancy, all the way to when we walk out of the door on our last day, or perhaps even beyond that with our interactions with

FIGURE 9.1 The different elements of job crafting

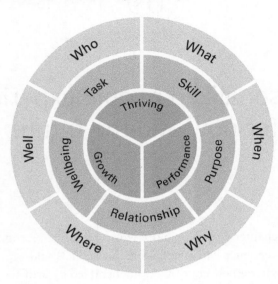

alumni networks and groups. An organization with a commitment to creating an exceptional employee experience becomes focused on how the individual can shape their interactions and experiences with the organization. Having opportunities to tailor and personalize work so that it aligns to the interests, values and needs of an individual are therefore fundamental in creating these positive employee experiences. Businesses which create these exceptional environments will enable employees to see that they are being valued and recognized as individuals. These workplaces will give people the trust, freedom and support to craft and create their work in ways that allow them to truly fulfil their potential in ways which will positively reverberate around their company.

When Professor Frank Piller, who we introduced in Chapter 1, talks about the benefits of mass customization and personalization from a manufacturing perspective, one of the key advantages he highlights, in addition to reduced costs and an improved user experience, is a reduction in waste.[1] In the case of fashion retail, there is an estimated £30 billion worth of clothes that sits unused and unworn in wardrobes across the UK. Research by EY[2] has found that nearly a quarter of all online clothing purchases have been returned by shoppers. Many of these returns don't make it back into circulation, meaning that in some instances retailers are in effect mass-producing waste. The reason that clothes remain unworn or are returned is that they don't ultimately fulfil the needs of the buyers in terms of colour, style or fit. Professor Piller's argument is that if customers are able to customize and make choices about the design of a product it's more likely that their individual preferences and desires will be met. Added to this, the process of designing and commissioning the design is also likely to positively raise an individual's investment in, and affinity with, the item when it finally arrives. When people build or create something they are much more likely to value it compared with something that they have been given. So in the case of clothes, they are much less likely to languish on the coat hanger if they have been personalized in some way.

Similarly, in the world of work, personalization enables us to prevent wastage in the form of talent and human potential. By encouraging and enabling people to customize and actively shape elements of their jobs, our energy, ideas and effort are also less likely to remain untapped, unused and unexplored in workplaces around the world.

Personalization at work not only raises contribution and effort, it also minimizes the costs associated with turnover and sickness. Table 9.1 shows some of the benefits of mass personalization in industry and the likely related benefits of a personalized approach to work in the workplace.

Unfortunately, we know that rather than embracing opportunities for people to customize and personalize their work, most organizations adopt what in manufacturing terms would be referred to as 'mass production' in terms of the way jobs are designed and performed and the choices people are able to make about how their work is structured and rewarded. Of course, it doesn't and shouldn't have to be this way and there are a number of ways that organizations can pursue a more personalized people agenda. The first step to doing this is to understand and explore what leads to personalization in the first instance.

TABLE 9.1 The benefits of personalization in industry and the workplace

Personalization in industry	Personalization in workplaces
Increased customer connection, engagement and loyalty	Higher levels of employee engagement, satisfaction and performance
Reduction in wastage	Reduction in turnover and performance management
Reduced supply chain costs	Reduced recruitment costs
Increased profitability by value pricing	Increased productivity and profitability

A formula for personalization

Personalization = choice + opportunity + energy

For organizations who want to explore and potentially increase opportunities for people to personalize and customize their work experiences there are three factors that they need to focus on and consider: choice, opportunity and energy.

Choice

In order to personalize any aspect of work, people need to have options or choices available to them. Choice and flexibility are, of course, on a spectrum, which ranges from no choice at all to full customization and total flexibility. In the case of working patterns, for example, some organizations may have no option or choice in terms of the hours that are worked, whilst other companies may allow people to effectively design their own working schedules and patterns, or even have no policy or stipulations regarding hours worked at all.

Whilst it might seem obvious, when designing choices it is important to consider what options people actually value and want. Rather than having choices made for others by senior leaders or shaped by systems and processes, organizations can demonstrate a commitment to a personalized employee experience through involving people in informing appropriate options and choices. Demonstrating this commitment to listening, understanding and responding to what people actually want is a visible and positive sign that the organization cares about creating an environment where employees have voice and an opportunity to contribute and create solutions.

Opportunity

Having choice and flexibility is, in most cases, beneficial but it won't mean anything if the choices available are hidden, complex, burdensome or not supported. Just because, for example, someone has the opportunity to choose it doesn't mean that that they will actively feel empowered to do it. The choices available to people need to be as clear as possible. For example, in the case of maternity or paternity leave the options available to mothers and fathers should not be buried in the depths of a policy or the head of an HR adviser, they should be communicated as openly and plainly as possible.

This transparency and clarity is important, because people won't select options that they don't know about and similarly are unlikely to make a choice if it is difficult to navigate and understand the full implications.

People are also unlikely to make a choice if it is not genuinely supported by the organization, irrespective of what is written in a policy. For example, I once worked in a team where a manager 'jokingly' chided a colleague who worked from home on a Friday with the comment, 'Are you shirking from home tomorrow as normal?' Whilst the comment might have been said in jest – and I have don't believe the manager deliberately did this to upset or provoke – it gave a clear signal to that colleague and others of us in the meeting that in reality working from home was not valued or supported despite what the organization's commitment to flexible working might have been.

Organizations need to think carefully about how they support employees to make the most of the options and flexibility available to personalize their jobs, working arrangements and their reward. Factors which could boost the levels of support available for employees could include training for managers, guidance and communications, an intranet site that's easy to access and navigate, and one-to-one support either face to face, by phone, instant message or even AI-enabled chatbot.[3]

Energy

Energy, or a lack of it, is often presented as a key reason for decision inertia and our status quo bias[4] when it comes to making choices and changing our circumstances. We are unlikely to be proactive and make active decisions if we don't have the time and energy to do so. Returning to the example of paternity leave, if an organization genuinely wanted to encourage greater parity between males and females taking leave then it could be more proactive in the support and encouragement it gave to prospective parents, and fathers in particular, to understand the options, support and opportunities available to them. This support could include clear guidance, case studies sharing stories of fathers taking leave, making connections with other fathers who have taken extended paternity leave, and providing access for a one-to-one meeting with an HR specialist to understand and explore the logistical and financial steps involved. From an energy perspective, employers could give prospective parents half a day's leave designed to give them space and the opportunity to plan, explore and talk over the logistics and options available with a partner, friend or family member.

POSITIVE ACTIONS FOR HR LEADERS IN PROMOTING A PERSONAL
EMPLOYEE EXPERIENCE

In order to evaluate and boost a more positive employee experience there are a
number of steps HR leaders can take:

- Audit the amount of choice and flexibility there is available across the
  employee experience.

- Identify any areas for investigation – where do people appear to be making
  the most or least of the choices available?

- Determine the amount of support available in making different choices – is
  there clear guidance? Is there visible leadership support? Are there stories of
  people making similar choices? Are managers supportive?

- Consider where and whether more choice and flexibility can and should be
  offered.

- Involve people from across the organization in the decision-making process
  when options are being considered and developed.

I'm not arguing that every element of the employee experience could and
should be actively personalized. Anyone who struggles to navigate the
options and customization choices available at a modern coffee shop will
understand how exhausting infinite options in the workplace would be.
Standardization, or deliberately limiting the choices available in many
aspects of our work, certainly helps both the employer and the employee.
You would, for example, need to think carefully about encouraging people
to customize or choose different internal messaging and communication
platforms, where there are clear benefits in terms of sharing and gathering
organizational knowledge if everyone uses the same shared tool. Similarly,
there may be certain advantages in offering a limited number of shift patterns
to customer-facing employees, who need to provide critical coverage and
support at certain times.

One area where HR needs to be more vigilant in particular is in checking
that the opportunities provided to personalize work keep pace with technological developments. Options that were created ten, five or even one year
ago may not reflect the current level of opportunities available to employees
and their organization. For example, in the case of reward and pay, most
organizations will offer no choice or flexibility in respect of when people are

paid. With digitization of bank transfers, new reward and payroll systems such as Gusto are able to create opportunities for flexible pay, where employees can personalize and choose when they get paid. Using these systems, employees can decide to get paid weekly, monthly or make a request with the swipe or click of a button for an immediate payment of any outstanding work carried out since their last pay cheque. There might be positives and negatives associated with introducing this scheme; they should be explored rather than being ignored. Technology also creates opportunities to change when and where we work. There is, for example, no need for customer service workers to be plugged into a headset in a call centre; technology now enables people to do this type of work remotely and consequently be more flexible in terms of the shifts they work. Again, there are considerations that need to be made about the type and level of flexibility that suits an organization and their customers, but the opportunities shouldn't be ignored.

Job crafting and a personalized people experience

Whether or not organizations need to actively offer employees the choice to craft is an interesting question. We know job crafting is employee-led and people tend to craft whether they have an active mandate or not, but it is also clear that crafting is more powerful and beneficial – both for the individual and the organization – when they do it openly 'in plain sight' rather than furtively hidden from the view of their manager. I would argue that everyone has the choice to craft, but I also recognize that many people don't feel or realize that the opportunity to proactively change or shape aspects of their job is available to them. The reason that people don't recognize job crafting as a choice comes down to opportunity and energy.

Role requirements, training and support, attitudes and leadership styles, and workplace culture more broadly undoubtedly shape the amount and type of job crafting that an employee makes. People are more likely to openly craft if they are encouraged by their managers to experiment with personalizing their work, if their leaders share stories of how they have done this, and if people feel safe to ask questions, make false steps, and try different approaches.

People are also more likely to craft if they have the energy and capacity to do so. Crafting is possible if people are stressed and strung out but the impact is diminished. In these circumstances, employees are more likely to use job crafting as a crutch or coping mechanism rather than in generative and positive ways. There are certainly things that HR professionals and people leaders can do to create more energy and opportunities to allow people to personalize and customize their work, and I hope that the research, ideas and case studies shared throughout this book and in Chapters 6, 7 and 8 specifically are a source of practical use and inspiration.

Just hands or whole humans?

In Chapter 1 I opened with a quote from Henry Ford and explained how his command and control approach to management thinking can still be seen alive and well in workplaces today. As we come to end of this book, another quote attributed to Henry Ford warrants consideration and exploration. Lamenting the challenge of working with humans and not machines, Ford is said to have asked (p 60):[5]

Why is it every time I ask for a pair of hands, they come with a brain attached?

Ford would surely be excited by the opportunities that are being presented by robotics and autonomation and the mechanization and excerebration of jobs. I once again disrespectfully disagree with Ford. I firmly believe that the purpose of work is not about controlling people but setting them free. Work should not be focused solely on the value, skills and tasks that people undertake. Employees should be given opportunities to contribute in meaningful and enriching ways which enable them to craft their own personal path to using their strengths and delivering excellence. Rather than attempting to quieten or mute the individuality of its employees – as we explored in Chapter 4 – there are lasting advantages in letting people craft and personalize their roles. This dials up and amplifies the diversity of talents, passions, interests and experiences that sit within each workplace. The benefits of a personalized approach to work are felt not just by employees, but by colleagues, leaders, customers, board members and shareholders too.

We need to be deliberate in how we embrace and use technology to shape our working lives. There are signs that we are already sleepwalking into the passive acceptance of technology automating tasks without stopping to think carefully about the rewards and costs of doing this from an individual, organizational or societal perspective. A case in point is the aviation industry, where flight technology is so advanced that autopilot now does as much as 90 per cent of the flying on a routine flight.[6] As Nicholas Carr argues in his book *The Glass Cage*,[7] computers have now taken over the cockpit.

Whilst technology has certainly delivered a number of advantages on the flight deck it has had a number of unintended consequences, particularly in relation to pilot skill. A 2011 Federal Aviation Authority (FAA) study[8] examined over 46 major accidents and over 700 reports that were voluntarily submitted by pilots in addition to data collected from over 9,000 flights. The report found that in over 60 per cent of accidents and 30 per cent of major incidents, pilots were found to have had problems physically flying the plane or had made errors with automated controls. In response to the report, Rory Kay, an airline captain and co-chair of the FAA committee on pilot training, warned that pilots were suffering from 'automation addiction' and that fundamentally pilots were 'forgetting how to fly'.[9] Similar findings were made in 2013 by the FAA, which concluded that 'Pilots sometimes rely too much on automated systems and may be reluctant to intervene' (p 36).[10] In response to these findings the FAA have recommended[11] that pilots take control of the plane more often and routinely practise flying aspects of flights manually to continue to maintain and strengthen their skills. As Earl Weiner, a leading authority on aviation has said, 'Digital devices tune out small errors while creating opportunities for large errors'.[12] Whilst technology is fantastic at performing standard tasks and operations, it is less able to respond to irregular and unpredictable hazards. Creative problem solving and flexible thinking are needed at these times. This, as demonstrated by Chesley Sullenberger when he famously landed US Airways Flight 1549 on the Hudson River in New York in 2009, is exactly where humans excel.

It's not just in the skies that automation and technology are shaping our mental capacities, and not always in a good way. Outsourcing remembering facts to a search engine or failing to form mental geographical maps of our locations and movements through a reliance on GPS navigation are just two examples of where we are not being cognitively stretched and tested in ways that we used to be. Psychologists have used the term digital dementia[13] to describe impairment to our cognitive abilities and capacities through an over-reliance on technology. From a work perspective, a reduction in cognitive challenge and stimulation is an important consideration as it has the potential to have a negative impact on our mental health, particularly as we age. Enriched work has been found to be linked to intellectual dexterity and cognitive functions as we get older[14,15,16] and a Swedish study[17] of over 10,000 twins found that complex and challenging work could reduce cognitive loss and specifically the risk of Alzheimer's disease.

A new work horizon

Eight-five per cent of the jobs that will exist in 2030 haven't been invented yet, according to a report commissioned by the Institute for the Future.[18] If this statistic is to believed, and this is the view of global technology, business and academic specialists, then there is tremendous opportunity for the world of work, HR, OD and work design. There is a fundamental opportunity for us to course correct in terms of the legacy of poorly designed jobs and uninspiring and unproductive work which many of us are living through, the roots of which can be traced back to the late 1800s.

The legacy of the decisions we make today in terms of work and organizational design, in the midst of a fourth Industrial Revolution, have the potential to be long lasting. As we've seen, the fallout and half-life of these types of decisions are considerable, with management practices and standards developed at the birth of mass production and manufacturing nearly 120 years ago still reverberating around workplaces today. Today's decisions about work and organizational design will therefore likely have a generational impact that will be felt not only in our own work and life experiences, but also in those of our children and even our children's children.

There is no doubt that technology will reshape the landscape of work, but that doesn't have to be at the detriment of humans. A number of studies and reports give us reason to be optimistic about the potential of technology to enrich work.[19,20,21,22] As machines take over predictable and repeatable aspects of work, the true value of automation and artificial intelligence will not be the ability to replace people with robots, but in augmenting the workforce and enabling the human components of work to be refocused on areas where they can make the strongest contribution in terms of problem solving, creativity and furthering knowledge, growth and development. By removing routine tasks, jobs have the potential to become more, rather than less, human and will enable the prominence and the value of people in work to increase in significance and value. Ultimately, technology will make personalization of work and job crafting easier and more assessible too. If there is no need to standardize or regulate a task – because that element of work is being done by technology – then people become free to carry out their work in less defined and more customizable ways.

Questions we need to ask ourselves

Whilst there is undoubtedly the opportunity for technology to have a positive influence on our work, it is by no account inevitable. The advancements in AI and automation could and can be used to eliminate and impoverish rather than augment and enrich the jobs we do.

People leaders and HR professionals will be pivotal in influencing the debate about the future of work design and how to embrace technology. Fundamentally, we need to ask ourselves some key questions:

- Do we want to amplify or strip out humanity from the workplace?
- Do we want work to further enslave us, or set us free?
- Do we use technology to further diminish or enrich our working lives?
- Do we fuse technology in our work to create 'super jobs' or do we cede control to the machines?
- Do we want to continue to mass produce and standardize or let people personalize and craft their jobs?
- Do we want to deliberately design work with mental health in mind?

Of course, I recognize these are leading questions. Well, at least I hope they are. And I know that the answers are not simply black and white. I'm realistic that there will always be some jobs that people will dread going to on a Monday morning and certain managers that will never have the confidence and trust to let their colleagues work autonomously and collaboratively. But I do believe that we can fundamentally flip the current depressing statistics where the vast majority of workers report being disengaged and dissatisfied with their work.[23,24] By taking a more personalized approach to work and organizational design we can create an environment where the majority of people are engaged and excited about their jobs and look forward to Monday mornings, or whenever and wherever their working day or week begins.

The opportunity to take a human-centred approach to work and organizational design has been with us for as long as work has existed. Whilst we can't unpick the past, we can start to frame our future. We are at a potential inflexion point where we can continue to find ever more advanced and ingenious ways to squeeze out the human dimension of work, or we can use technology as a stimulus to encourage personalized and employee-led ways of working that amplify what it means to be human and enable us to do jobs that are stimulating, meaningful, valuable and adaptable.

The decisions we make about the nature of work that organizations want to create and how they want to use technology must involve HR and people leaders. A seat at the 'top table' for HR is no longer good enough. Rather than just being part of the strategic conversation, HR need to lead it. It will be only through a position of strategic influence that HR are able to effectively steer their organizations and their industries into making decisions to invest and implement technological solutions in ways that enable people to flourish rather than flounder.

The legacy of these types of decisions could, as it has done in the past, remain with us for hundreds of years. Wouldn't it be amazing if we made a commitment to radically change our relationship with and perceptions of 'work' so that rather than being something we endured it was instead something to be savoured? What if work was seen as something that positively contributed to, rather than got in the way of, our 'real' lives?

What do you believe?

Fundamentally, the decisions and actions you take in terms of the current and future design of work will be based on your perceptions of people and the contribution you feel employees can truly make.

And so, as you finish this book, I have a question for you. What do you believe is the contribution that people can truly make to your organization, and their potential to do so?

If you believe that employees can't be trusted, need to be controlled, are not interested in work and are only there for a pay cheque, you will undoubtedly make decisions and create a workplace where this is the case. For people who believe this, I hope that the ideas and research in this book allow you at least to understand the limitations and costs, from both human and performance perspectives, of this approach.

For those leaders and HR professionals who believe, as I do, that people naturally strive to positively collaborate, meaningfully contribute and add value, then you will create an environment where this happens. You will naturally be curious about how to enable colleagues across your company to do their best work, in ways that bring their passions, talents and strengths to life. If you believe in, and are committed to, creating working environments and jobs where people can bring their whole and best selves to work, I hope that the ideas in this book will fuel your curiosity and give you practical ideas to craft and explore. That would truly be personalization at work.

KEY POINTS

- To create a personalized people experience employees need choice, opportunity and energy to shape their work.

- Technological innovations such as AI, robotics and automation have the potential to both positively enrich and negatively impoverish work.

- HR leaders have a pivotal responsibility and role in shaping organizational decisions around how technology is introduced.

QUESTIONS

- How will technology such as automation, AI and robotics shape and influence your organization?

- To what extent do you and your organization recognize and fundamentally believe in the value that people can make to your business – now and in the future?

- How can you influence decisions and conversations about how technological innovations are brought into your organization, and are you doing so?

Notes

1 Piller, F T, Moeslein, K and Stotko, C M (2004) Does mass customization pay? An economic approach to evaluate customer integration, *Production Planning & Control*, **15** (4), pp 435–44

2 EY (2016) Nearly a quarter of online clothing purchases returned by shoppers, available at: https://www.ey.com/uk/en/newsroom/ (archived at https://perma.cc/3D49-2PZN), or go to https://www.b4-business.com/press-releases/nearly-a-quarter-of-online-clothing-purchases-returned-by-shoppers/ (archived at https://perma.cc/A6RR-KBMA)

3 Parlo (2018) 7 ways chatbot and AI are disrupting HR, *Chatbots Magazine*, available at: https://chatbotsmagazine.com/7-ways-chatbots-and-ai-are-disrupting-hr-3989ad1c1fed (archived at https://perma.cc/4LLS-VZ8D)

4 Samuelson, W and Zeckhauser, R J (1988) Status quo bias in decision making, *Journal of Risk and Uncertainty*, **1**, pp 7–59

5 Semler, R (2004) *The Seven-day Weekend: A better way to work in the 21st century*, Random House, p 60

6   Smith, O (2017) Confessions of an airline pilot, *Telegraph*, available at: https://www.telegraph.co.uk/travel/travel-truths/confessions-of-an-airline-pilot/ (archived at https://perma.cc/XGB5-KJA6)

7   Carr, N (2015) *The Glass Cage: Where automation is taking us*, Random House

8   CBS News (2011) Study: automatic pilot may add to flight risk, available at: https://www.cbsnews.com/news/study-automatic-pilot-may-add-to-flight-risk/ (archived at https://perma.cc/WSZ8-LLNP)

9   Orr, J (2011) Airline pilots 'so reliant on computers they forget how to fly', *Telegraph*, available at: https://www.telegraph.co.uk/finance/newsbysector/ industry/8732414/Airline-pilots-so-reliant-on-computers-they-forget-how-to-fly.html (archived at https://perma.cc/J3DD-ZZTC)

10   FAA (2013) Operational use of flight path management systems, available at: https://www.faa.gov/aircraft/air_cert/design_approvals/human_factors/media/ OUFPMS_Report.pdf (archived at https://perma.cc/74EW-VAAU)

11   Nicas, J and Wichter, Z (2019) A worry for some pilots: their hands-on flying skills are lacking, *New York Times*, available at: https://www.nytimes. com/2019/03/14/business/automated-planes.html (archived at https://perma.cc/ KPK8-Z4EY)

12   Harford, T (2016) Crash: how computers are setting us up for disaster, *Guardian*, available at: https://www.theguardian.com/technology/2016/oct/11/ crash-how-computers-are-setting-us-up-disaster (archived at https://perma.cc/ 6BVN-359W)

13   Greenfield, S (2015) Digital dementia: video games improve attention, but is there also a link with dementia? *Psychology Today*, available at: https://www. psychologytoday.com/gb/blog/mind-change/201507/digital-dementia# targetText=%E2%80%9CDigital%20Dementia%E2%80%9D%20is%20 a%20term,underuse%20if%20we%20overuse%20technology (archived at https://perma.cc/TCF9-A2XW)

14   Parker, S K (2014) Beyond motivation: job and work design for development, health, ambidexterity, and more, *Annual Review of Psychology*, 65, pp 661–91

15   Karp A *et al* (2009) Mentally stimulating activities at work during midlife and dementia risk after age 75: follow-up study from the Kungsholmen Project, *American Journal of Geriatric Psychiatry*, 17, pp 227–36

16   Schooler C, Mulatu, M S and Oates, G (2004) Occupational self-direction, intellectual functioning, and self-directed orientation in older workers: findings and implications for individuals and societies, *American Journal of Sociology*, 110, pp 161–97

17   Andel, R *et al* (2005) Complexity of work and risk of Alzheimer's disease: a population-based study of Swedish twins, *The Journals of Gerontology Series B: Psychological Sciences and Social Sciences*, 60 (5), pp P251–P258

18 Institute for the Future and Dell Technologies (2017) The next era of human/machine partnerships, available at: https://www.delltechnologies.com/content/dam/delltechnologies/assets/perspectives/2030/pdf/SR1940_IFTFforDellTechnologies_Human-Machine_070517_readerhigh-res.pdf (archived at https://perma.cc/Q9AG-9LAM)

19 Volini, E *et al* (2019) From jobs to superjobs: 2019 global human capital trends, Deloitte, available at: https://www2.deloitte.com/us/en/insights/focus/human-capital-trends/2019/impact-of-ai-turning-jobs-into-superjobs.html#targetText=New%20research%20shows%20that%20the,communication%2C%20service%2C%20and%20collaboration (archived at https://perma.cc/VX2F-9ZCC)

20 CIPD (2019) People and machines: from hype to reality, available at: https://www.cipd.co.uk/Images/people-and-machines-report-1_tcm18-56970.pdf (archived at https://perma.cc/8533-W2PD)

21 World Economic Forum (2016) The Future of Jobs, available at: http://www3.weforum.org/docs/WEF_Future_of_Jobs.pdf (archived at https://perma.cc/9PTK-HUVB)

22 Balfe, N, Sharples, S and Wilson, J R (2015) Impact of automation: measurement of performance, workload and behaviour in a complex control environment, *Applied Ergonomics*, 47 (C), pp 52–64

23 Gallup (2017) State of the Global Workplace, available at: https://www.gallup.com/workplace/238079/state-global-workplace-2017.aspx (archived at https://perma.cc/2SHK-HMEC)

24 Hayes, M *et al* (2018) The Global Study of Engagement, *ADP*, available at: https://www.adp.com/-/media/adp/resourcehub/pdf/adpri/adpri0100_2018_engagement_executive_summary_release%20ready.ashx (archived at https://perma.cc/PN5K-CYNP)

INDEX